PUPPETS AND PERFORMING OBJECTS

A PRACTICAL GUIDE

PUPPETS AND PERFORMING OBJECTS

A PRACTICAL GUIDE

TINA BICÂT

THE CROWOOD PRESS

First published in 2007 by
The Crowood Press Ltd
Ramsbury, Marlborough
Wiltshire SN8 2HR

www.crowood.com

Front cover image: Venus from the Royal Shakespeare Company/Little Angel Theatre Company production of *Venus and Adonis*. Photograph by Robert Day. Copyright Royal Shakespeare Company
Back cover image: scene from St Mary's University College production of *Nothing Compares to You*. Photograph by Alistair Milne

British Library Cataloguing-in-Publication Data
A catalogue record for this book is available from the British Library.

ISBN 978 1 86126 960 7

Typeset by Carolyn Griffiths

Printed and bound in India by Replika Press

CONTENTS

THANKS

My thanks to everyone who talked to me about their work, let me see and photograph their work-in-progress and let me use their photographs, and to everyone who helped me, including: Alison King, Alistair Milne, Amsterdam's Marionetten Theater, Amy Bicât, Arthur Bird, Au Cul du Loup, Bernd Kessler, Brigitte Lambert, Carolina Ruiz Marcos, Caroline Sharman, Charlotte Cunningham, Chris Baldwin, Daniel Erice, Derek Nisbet, Drak company in Hradec Kralove, Institut International de la Marionette in Charleville-Mezières, Felix Barrett, 'The Firebird' company at the Stephen Joseph Theatre, Fred Abels, Fred is Dead company, Gren Middleton, Mark Griffin, Hendrik Bonnheur, Improbable Theatre, the Scottish National Theatre and the 'Wolves in the Walls' company, Indefinite Articles, Josephine Machon, Puy Delgardo, Jonathan McDonnell, Julian Crouch, Juliet Rogers, Kasia Zeremba-Byrne, Kate Bicât, la Famille Magnifique, Laurie Sanson, Lee Threadgold, Libby Northedge, Lyndie Wright, Mar Mateo, Maria Oshodi, Marta Gomara Miramon, Maxine Doyle, Mirjam Langemeijer, Nick Bicât, Ockham's Razor, Penny Embden, Peter Charlton, Rebecca Middleton, Roman Stefanski, Ruth Naylor-Smith, Sally Brown, Steve Horne, Steve Tiplady, Tallerspiral, the Drama and Physical Theatre students and staff of St Mary's University College, Twickenham, the Little Angel Theatre, Tony Bicât and Trevor Walker.

All photographs in the book are by the author unless otherwise stated.

The terms 'he' and 'she' are used indiscriminately throughout the book as everyone does everything in the world of puppets and objects.

Love to my brothers Tony and Nick Bicât without whom... ...

INTRODUCTION

This book explores how inventors and performers make and use puppets, objects, shadows and visual effects, and create theatre using these inanimate objects. Many of their most successful inventions are so simple that it can seem impossible that they are able to bring a complex, adult character to life. Yet in the right hands a clothes peg could play Hitler and chill the audience with its performance. Folk literature has many examples of the Puppet Master, a strange and often rather demonic figure who dictates and rules the lives of his troop. Their struggle to free their emotions from their wooden bodies demonstrates our consciousness that the spirit in a puppet or object when it comes to life on stage has a magical and perhaps a dangerous quality. But it is not always so solemn. Puppets and objects, and the double bluff they play on us that makes us believe and not believe at the same time, can make some of the funniest possible moments on any stage. We may not understand why it works, but we know, when we are absorbed in the life that these pretend-people and transforming objects play out for us, that it does.

The power of puppets to tell a story and transmit emotion to an audience has been used since the earliest theatre, though much of the instinctive, serious attention given to this art form slipped away over time. In many countries the work became thought of as less of an art form and more of a device used for children's entertainment. The trend towards naturalism in theatre performance made the use of puppets seem out of place. However, towards the end of the twentieth century and in the beginning of our present one, many theatre productions have pulled away both from naturalism and narrative theatre. Puppets and objects, lively and anarchic in the inventive hands of their operators, have leapt up and grabbed the opportunity to give stories and emotions to the audience in all sorts of performance.

The word 'puppet' still conjures up, to many people, a marionette or a glove puppet used to tell simplistic stories to children. The term 'visual theatre', which is used more in other areas of Europe than in Britain, gives perhaps a more true idea of the nature of the work. Puppets can pack a powerful intellectual, political and emotional punch, subtle enough for the most complex work for children but strong and serious enough for the most adult drama.

It is relatively easy to talk about puppets and for everyone to understand you. However,

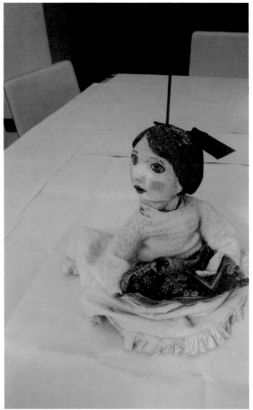

Puppets tell all sorts of stories.
a) Beautiful Adonis, a marionette from the Royal Shakespeare and the Little Angel Theatre Company's Venus and Adonis by Shakespeare.

b) Kate Bicât's Vasalisa, a little girl from the Russian folk tale for children.

A ventilation tube fitted with an accordion-style valve that sings to the audience as it dances (Au Cul du Loup).

Students playing with objects in rehearsal.

performing objects and their use in object theatre are less familiar to many people and therefore need more explanation. The two are closely related. The invention of these performing objects – these sets, props or costumes, which can adopt and relinquish character through the way they are used – demand that the creator looks at their design from a new perspective. Conventional props are made to look and behave as much like the real thing as possible; for example, a prop broadsword will not be sharp and will not have the same weight as a real one. The metal, resin, wood or whatever it is made of will be decorated to look as convincing as possible. The two-handed chop of the actor as he slaughters his opponent will convince the audience of its weight and efficiency as a killing weapon. The designer and maker will have read the script, studied the character and status of the sword's owner, done the research, drawn the object, had it made and given it to the actor to work with, possibly under the

tuition of a fight director who is an expert in fighting technique and its history. The maker of a broadsword for object theatre will approach the creation of this sword via another path.

The company will sit in rehearsal and watch the actor, who uses a stick to represent the sword, and recreate the use of the stick as rehearsals proceed. The object will stay ostensibly a sword. But maker, director and actor will not know how it will perform before they start: the idea is not fixed, the possibilities are open and there is room for invention by anyone in the company. The object may relate to the set, the costume or the props, as well as to the actor who uses it.

There is more to these objects than appears at first sight and the expectations the audience is likely to have of these objects may be confounded. Think of 'Lion', that rather unrewarding role for Snug the Joiner in Shakespeare's *A Midsummer Night's Dream*. Snug could be dressed in a pantomime lion

9

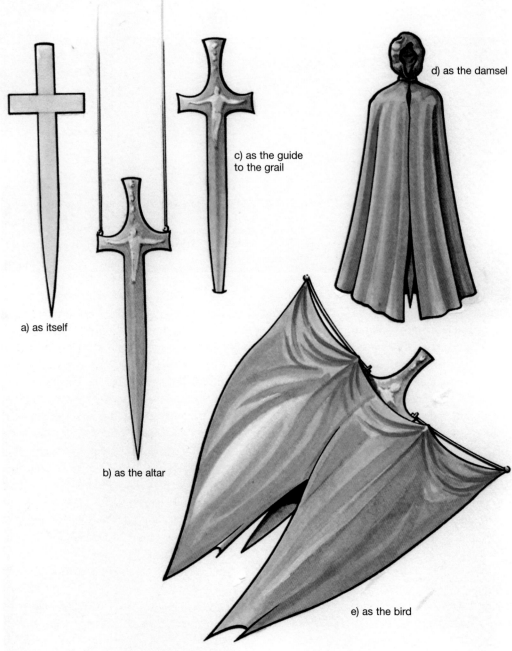

d) as the damsel

c) as the guide
to the grail

a) as itself

b) as the altar

e) as the bird

The transformation of a broadsword.

It could happen like this ...

The object may not be required to be only a sword. But perhaps:

- the cross of the guard should be slightly exaggerated and a hole made in the stage floor so that it can become an altar
- it could have cloth draped over the crosspiece shoulders of its guard and become the puppet damsel the knight is fighting for
- the decoration of the hilt could conceal hooks for the mechanism that will make it hover in the air and lead the knight to the grail
- the guard could allow for the attachment of wings so that it can become a bird that takes the message back to the damsel, its alter ego.

It will still, through all these adaptations, be to the audience a recognizable broadsword. Its journey from stick to transforming object would use the skills of director, actor, designer, musician and maker. Written down, this may sound like a fanciful concoction of ideas that would convince nobody. But take the time really to imagine this changeable sword within its story onstage with an open mind.

costume. He could be dressed in his ordinary labourer's costume and have a sign saying 'Lion' dangling round his neck. Or he could have been mopping the stage, whip the top off the mop, which has been adapted to make a lion's mane, and use the empty central section where the mop head would attach to its stick as a hand-held animated big mouth when he gives his spectacular ROAR. The object used would appear to be an ordinary mop head but would have been adapted to suit its dual purpose as lion mane-and-mouth and cleaning device. It would maintain a homemade feeling in keeping with the spirit of the gym-crack skills of that group of Bottom's players.

The actors who use transforming objects in their work tend not to be trained puppeteers, though they may come from a training that has involved work with movement, masks, circus or another physical theatre and are easy with the idea of improvisation and devised theatre. The distinction between 'props' and 'objects' is in the way they are used. The object in object theatre has a life outside the use for which its non-theatrical inventor intended and it does not have to obey the rules of physics and gravity. It has a magic to help it perform in extraordinary ways; a magic made by actors, animators, designers and the audience.

The workroom in action.

1. THE CONVENTIONS OF PUPPET THEATRE

WHY PUPPETS?

The Changing Audience

Puppets have edged their way onto mainstream stages and into performances with gentle and inexorable persistence. A previous generation of theatre-goers might have been surprised by the sight of a puppet appearing, unadvertised, in a cast full of humans and might have been resistant to its impact upon their emotions. Now these subtle creatures mingle with actors and add a new dimension to the drama. It is difficult to pinpoint why this change has taken place and why, after so many years in the wings of adult theatre, puppets have achieved a credibility and status as performers, which previously they had only been given by fervent fans of the genre. The most likely answer seems to be rooted in the practice of encouraging audiences to trust their own imaginations, which is encouraged by the object and visual theatre of today.

Why Use Puppets?

There is no realism onstage. No performance can be realistic. Even the truest-to-life soap opera or fly-on-the-wall documentary is a matter of lighting and costume, budget battles, contracts signed, lines learnt and sets built. Puppets and objects in performance display this fact most blatantly. A man who is an actor can play Hamlet; he could, given the right circumstances, be a real prince and actually die onstage. But a 30cm (12in) high Hamlet of wood, paper and cloth cannot be heir to Elsinore. The audience knows he is not a human with bones and blood. There is no pretence from the stage. They agree to put doubts and prejudices away till later and collude with the theatrical experience.

And because of this, as in an abstract painting or a piece of music, the audience's emotions are directly engaged without having to travel through a mist of apparent naturalism. The heart and imagination of the most prosaic audience member can be moved by an object of fabric and glue. Everything and anything becomes possible and believable. A 3m (118in) tall man made of sellotape can ford a wide and shining river of clingfilm and sow the imaginary seeds of a new settlement.

Close beside the artistic and creative advantages of puppets lies their practicality and versatility. They can be small, cheap and easily transportable and can tell any story to anyone more or less anywhere. They have had their difficulties edging into adult performance but are very resilient, and thanks to those who

It could happen like this ...

A performance of a Mozart opera. The audience waits for it to begin in the elegant little theatre. Some of the adults who accompany their children assume that a puppet performance must be aimed at the children rather than them. They assume that the marionettes will not give them the satisfying experience they expect from such music. For the first few minutes of the performance this seems to be true and then a transformation happens. The strings of the marionettes cease to matter. The unreality of the movement of the characters begins to produce a direct connection with the music and its rhythms. The purity and emotional frankness inherent in the music seems uncluttered by the extraneous emotion that any human performer must give to a characterization. The characters seem much closer to the source of the music, even though it is emanating from singers and musicians who are not performing on the stage. The dialogue is between the music and the audience. The jokes in the music are funny; the love story genuinely touching. Puppet characters and the listeners interpret it together. At the end of the opera, the company takes a bow and the stage clears. And onto the stage comes Mozart himself; not an actor dressed as Mozart but a puppet Mozart who by this time seems real and the audience has the singular experience of applauding the creator of this wonderful work.

For further information about the Amsterdam Marionette Theatre, visit www.marionettentheater.nl

'The wooden actors take the audience into a world where magic lives on; a world which reminds us of the lost innocence of childhood.' Hendrik Bonneur, producer/director of the Amsterdam Marionette Theatre, here shown on the bridge of the stage. Photo: Datema and Mulder

A cork is given a character by simple and effective means.

Maker at work on a puppet that can open its body in performance.

believe in their power to tell all sorts of stories, they pop up in mainstream adult theatre everywhere.

A puppet is by nature impassive. It contains the possibility to display all sorts of emotion but it can't do it alone. It needs us in order to live. Its very impassivity pushes us towards questions and truths which engross philosophers and children. Its bloodless, blameless body allows us the freedom to laugh or cry at it and with it. Its life does not exist without the one who animates it and the one who watches it.

Most people who work with puppets and objects create work that needs the abstraction from reality that puppets allow. Puppet drama is not the same as drama performed by humans. It is not merely that anything is physically possible to a puppet: its body can open to reveal its beating heart; it can fly and function without oxygen; it can transform and shatter, change gender and species and abstract itself from our world's reality or be as cosy as buttered toast. It can do and be whatever is necessary to the plot.

The energy that travels from animator to object invests the puppet with the combined power of these two, plus that of the audience's imagination. This three-way exchange depends on the animator. Through his or her work, the creative output of the scriptwriter,

15

director, musicians and designers is passed on to the audience; the audience then connects with the puppet in a way that the familiar humanity of an actor does not permit.

Performing the Impossible

Puppets can be used to differentiate between species. Narratives in which angels and humans appear in the script or humans meet aliens from another planet, or in which humans share a story with animals or fairies are all obvious examples of times when puppets are a convenient answer to a casting problem. People would imagine fairies to be small – or a least smaller than humans, and rather less solid. Angels are big, perhaps even huge, and both fly – we all know that. Many mythical monsters are far bigger than the humans they threaten. Ghosts appear and disappear. So can the shadows of puppets and objects. Puppets can answer the practical problems of size and solidity in the creation of a production.

Puppets are also adept at showing the audience the complex inner worlds of the human mind. All the dreams, visions, fears and tricks our brains can invent are well within the compass of the puppet performer.

There is also the convenience of using puppets as babies or young children; apart from the impossibility of getting a reliable characterization from a three-month-old child, there are legal restrictions to children working on stage that won't apply to the puppet child. Anyone who has seen an unconvincing pillow-in-a-shawl babe-in-arms onstage will appreciate the advantage of using the slight movement that can be created by the actor placing a finger or hand in a simple pocket at the back of the prop-baby's head or on a

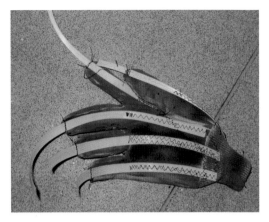

The far-reaching hand of death:
a) Under construction ...

b) ... ready to clutch.

limb, and moving it to bring the baby to life.

Puppet animals, too, are more reliable than real ones and come without the regulations and handlers that accompany performing animals. They have the same power to ensnare an audience's affection ('Never work with children or animals!'), but at least the animator must feel some of the glory. The relationship between a human actor and a puppet animal can seem just as loving and attractive to the

The slightest movement of an arm brings a puppet baby to life.

audience as that between an actor and a living dog.

TYPES OF PUPPET

It is difficult to categorize the hundreds of different puppets that exist. They often jostle and shift from one group to another but can be more or less divided into these groups. They won't stay in them. Puppeteers and makers use any technique of animation that works.

Stick Puppets

The most basic is a stick with a flat cut-out of a figure attached to it, which can be used to create shadows as well as direct effects. The hands that hold the stick and animate the puppet can be concealed behind a screen or piece of scenery.

Marionettes

Figures animated by strings controlled from above. In a sense, they are the most naturalistic puppets as the animators work at some distance from them and are usually invisible. Some are made with the most exquisite detail. The operation of many-stringed marionettes can be complex and some actions may require two or three puppeteers to activate an elaborate and natural-looking movement.

Glove Puppets

Glove puppets are limited in movement but have their own advantages. They can be fast and direct. They can grab and hit and hug. The movement of the hand can be synchronized with speech so that the puppet can 'talk'. The close and obvious physical proximity of the animator and the puppet leads to a particularly engaging relationship with the audience.

Rod Puppets

One hand holds the rod that supports the puppet and controls the movements of its head. The other hand controls the puppet's gestures by means of wires or sticks attached to the hands or direct hand-to-hand contact. The animator's own hand may be used in the sleeve of the puppet's costume on bigger puppets.

Bunraku

The traditional way to animate these large puppets is through three puppeteers who work together. They are visible but focus their attention on the puppet. One controls the head and the right hand, one the left hand and the third

Types of puppet.

the feet and the costume. All sorts of variations of this principle can be used, in which several people animate one figure.

Shadow Puppets

The image of the puppet is thrown onto a translucent screen by light. The puppets and light source can be behind or in front of the screen. This form of puppetry depends on the ability of people to recognize silhouettes and the way shadows become bigger or smaller depending on their distance from the light source. The sort of special effects and theatrical wizardry that belong to big budgets and technical equipment can be created by nothing more than a light source and silhouette.

Most of these categories overlap and change. New ideas are invented all the time and old ones are given a fresh perspective as

It could happen like this ...

Every year, a barge makes its way from its London home down the Thames. Its hold, where coal used to be carried, now contains an auditorium, a puppet stage and all the lighting and sound equipment needed to create a puppet show. It carries with it a tradition as old as theatre – the combination of stubborn belief in the work, dogged hard slog and the imaginative invention that has always inspired creators of theatre to find a way to present their ideas to the public. In this unlikely theatre, puppets perform for children and adults work which ranges from fairy stories to the great guns of literature. Children can delight in what may be their first experience of theatre as they watch the adventures of a puppet rabbit. Their parents can be given the opportunity to experience a fresh insight into Shakespeare or Lorca, or to view a specially commissioned play.

The transformation of the tiny stage occurs in the minds of the audience; the often jaded imagination of the habitual theatre-goer is startled back to the excitement and involvement of the things that first made them love theatre. They are prompted to flesh out the wooden bodies of the performers with all the character inherent in the role and become silent actors themselves by virtue of their involvement with the puppets onstage.

For further information about the Movingstage Marionette Company's Puppet Theatre Barge, visit www.puppetbarge.com

technology and the theatrical world change. The inventors, makers and animators all have their own passions and techniques for bringing their ideas to life, as well as their own theories of construction and animation. It is an art which lives, develops and changes without losing respect and affection for, and need of, its antecedents.

PERFORMANCE SPACES

It is not always necessary to have complicated arrangements – all sorts of puppet stages can be made from rostra and screens. A simple backcloth which reveals the puppeteers from the waist up and hides their feet whilst creating a background for the scene requires much less organization and expense than a permanent stage. Colour and lighting can determine the audience focus and guide its attention away from the puppeteers and onto the puppets. If the puppeteers are dressed in black and set against a black backcloth they will be ignored by the audience after the first few minutes of performance. It's worth noting that black fabric used for such backgrounds and costumes should be wool, cotton jersey or rough-weave cotton, that is, cloth which absorbs rather than reflects light; shiny black cloth will pick up the colour of the light and draw attention to the people you want to hide.

Theatres built specially for puppet performance differ from traditional theatre buildings. The size of the proscenium arch is smaller than that of a stage used by humans. Puppet stages have to allow for the practicality of concealing the puppeteer and showing the puppet to best advantage. The backstage arrangements are often complicated by the necessity of being able to hang or place puppets and props where they can be taken up easily and reliably to make their appearance onstage. Marionettes must hang from their controls so that their strings do not tangle and hand puppets must be placed so that there will not be any fumbling when they are taken up to perform.

Marionette Theatres

A traditional marionette theatre will have a platform-like bridge above the stage, usually concealed from the audience by a screen or false proscenium. The puppeteers can lean over the rail and look down on the marionettes performing in the stage light below them. Marionette companies that play in spaces not designed for their particular needs may travel with their portable bridge or screen if they need to work unseen by the audience. Such complications become necessary when sets are elaborate and the style of the piece demands that the puppeteers should be hidden.

Hand Puppet Stages

Hand and rod puppets, if their animators are to be concealed, need a different stage to work on, a ledge rather than a platform and wings which hide performers from the audience. The puppeteers will work below or beside the puppets and their bodies will be screened by the front of the stage or the wings. This stage can be a complicated proscenium arch with all the gilded trappings of a miniature opera house or a much more homely affair of a screen or cloth hanging over a pole in front of the puppeteers. Whatever the style, the purpose is the same – to give the puppets a place to perform where they can be seen clearly by the audience. It is often a matter of contrast. If the puppets blend into the background they won't show up as well. Texture and lighting are as important as colour; the light must catch the puppets in a more lively way than it affects the background, particularly if the puppets are small and the audience large.

19

A puppeteer crouching under the platform where her puppet performs.

Shadow Play

The stage of a shadow puppet play is really a screen. A light source casts the puppet's or object's shadow on a screen; the shadow is then seen by the audience. The screen must be translucent enough for the light to penetrate but taut enough to hang without folds, which would cause shadows.

Shadows can also be thrown onto the set from the audience's side of the footlights. A small object lit from the front can throw a huge shadow onto a stage wall or floor, acquiring a powerful second presence at the flick of a switch.

Touring Stages

There is a long tradition of the travelling puppet show; Mr Punch's and similar booths

A shadow man climbs a mountain at sunset. Photo: Mar Mateo

It could happen like this ...

There is to be a shadow puppet play in the village square. The excitement over this unusual event in such a rural situation has spread to surrounding villages and they want a performance too. The company, who have created a screen by making up a wooden frame of roofing battens that happened to be lying around and stapling a white sheet over it, have to think again. The light source comes from halogen security lights plugged in via a trailing extension lead through the window into a friendly local kitchen. The music is a man with a guitar. The equipment must be carried to the other venues in somebody's car and it won't fit.

The garden and agricultural supply shop has plastic-covered metal stakes which fit together with corner clips to make fruit cages and frames for beans to climb over. They are brought into use as a frame that can be easily dismantled. The white sheet has channels sewn along its borders so that the stakes can be threaded through before being fastened together. There is no need for seating; members of the audience bring their own chairs. Frame, puppets, lights and performers can all pack into the car and move to the village across the valley and make their magic again in another village plaza.

For further information about the site-specific performances of the Spanish troupe Spirál, visit www.tallerspiral.com

have been a familiar sight on streets and beaches and in parks for hundreds of years. Throughout the world, puppet companies continue to take their performances to the people in this way. There are certain advantages to the touring puppet company. The human members of the company may have to be fed and lodged, but the puppets are an uncomplaining lot and providing they are kept relatively clean and dry will do their job when called upon.

Puppet stages tour in many different guises, from the shelf that hangs round the neck, rather like an ice-cream vendor's tray, to the adapted caravan that unfolds into a magnificent stage and then folds up again after the performance and rolls on to the next venue. The Punch and Judy man's stage packs into a bundle of sticks and cloth or flat-pack boards, and the puppets travel in their boxes and bags to the next performance. Puppet festivals and street theatre have inspired puppeteers to create portable stages out of double basses, wheelbarrows, fish tanks or a simple little platform of wood strapped to a bent left forearm while the puppeteer animates the glove puppet with their right hand.

2. THE CONVENTIONS OF OBJECT THEATRE

It could happen like this ...

She is eating her lunch. The clock ticks, a dog barks outside and through the window we see gentle sunlight. She grinds pepper onto her food. The sound of the grinding pepper is amplified, making a noise like the rumble of a cart going past the window. The shadow of a cart passes the window. The tick of the clock turns into the regular stamping of a marching army, while the clock's hand jerks second by second to the tramp of the march. She stands, terrified, still holding the pepper pot, the shadow of which is now projected onto the stage to make the shape of a soldier in a helmet looming gigantic over the scene. It is the beginning of a story, and the story is not going to be about a pepper pot and a clock. The objects and shadows have adopted a new significance.

The description 'object theatre' is an attempt to name a style that imbues props and objects with particular significance. We have to call it something in order to talk about it. In the same way that other types of performance, such as melodrama or theatre of cruelty were named when they achieved prominence in their day, object theatre and visual theatre have become phrases that are familiar in the European theatrical and academic vocabulary. The impracticability of trying to name any genre comes, as always, from the fact that the ideas are never new and separate – it is the perspective of the protagonist and the audience that has shifted and made them appear so.

The great difficulty in talking about this genre of theatre comes from the vocabulary which surrounds it and tends to isolate it into a separate pocket of its own. It changes its name as often as its country and its genre. It belongs in, and breaks out into, all sorts of performance. Any production, classical or contemporary, which does not depend on an apparently naturalistic representation of real life can give these objects, these hybrids of props and puppets, the opportunity to help tell the story. As their use becomes more central to today's theatre, actors become more skilled in object manipulation and the fusing of the animation of objects into their characterizations.

OBJECTS OR PROPS?

The animal that speaks, the lamp that releases the genie, Pandora's Box and Cinderella's glass slipper have lived in our imaginations for so long that we almost forget they are the fruits of myth and impossibility and not solid fact. How

Simple props and costumes invested with strong associations. Photo: Alistair Milne

often do we imagine the mess of blood and pain that would become of a foot encased in a glass shoe? Hardly a romantic image. We have all seen terrifying shadows which turn out to be harmless objects, mere optical illusions. The power these objects exert on our imagination, and the ease with which members of the audience can believe the unbelievable when their own imaginations are engaged, is the strength behind the successful use of objects in performance.

Why Use Objects?

Much devised performance in contemporary theatre involves objects whose use and transformations during the telling of the story will be influenced by the actors who are using them. Objects, often created from the discarded leftovers of our everyday, life are given new significance and power by directors, designers and actors. Umbrellas become guns and ladders become monsters. The choice to use objects in this way is often linked to a need to take the work outside the confines of conventional reality to a more imaginative exploration of how humans tumble through lives, countries tumble through history and worlds tumble through the universe. Different forms of performance, once so separate, join together to become an animated way of giving life to a story. They play a considerable part in cutting-edge and student dramatic

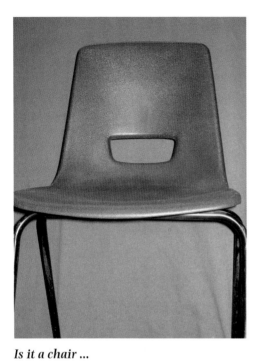 

Is it a chair ...   *... or is it a monster?*

A car is built onstage. Photo: Alistair Milne

performance today. Dance, acting, music, puppetry, mime, circus and installation overlap and blend.

Creative Collaboration

A naturalistic play, most scripted work, a film, a play or a ballet can be designed without direct input from the performers. The script can be read, the director can discuss decisions with the team and the designs can be drawn, approved and shopped for. Set building and prop making can begin and costume fittings take place before the performers have had their first day of rehearsal. They often arrive for their first day of work to find that the costumes, props and set will have already been settled and agreed between the director, designers and makers. There will be changes and alterations, but the basic concept will remain the same and depend little on what takes place during rehearsal.

Object and visual theatre cannot work like this; or if it does it will be losing creative company collaboration, its greatest, though often inconvenient, strength.

A Different Sort of Audience Involvement

Props have always been part of theatrical experience and those who make them and use them understand that they are rarely what they seem. The hangman's noose with its safety fastening of easily broken cotton thread and the drunkard with his whisky bottle of cold tea are old friends. Theatre has absorbed these tricks in its representations of reality and it doesn't take much effort from the audience to believe that the noose is real and the whisky alcoholic. After all, they look much the same. Objects used on stage have become more than just props.

Object or visual theatre shifts props into the spotlight and gives them an active and dramatic role in the action, most particularly in non-naturalistic drama and in performance where the interior life and secret world of the characters on-stage is discovered through what the audience sees, as much as the words it hears.

People who invent this sort of work lead their audience beyond the two-dimensional trick into a surreal world where nothing is what it seems. The humans onstage are joined by a cast of performing objects. The objects in these performances do not work in the same way as puppets, though they share many of the same virtues. They retain the appearance, attributes and behaviour of the things they represent and it is the skill of the animator and the imagination of the audience which make them seem to take their shape in the story onstage; a book may be used as a bird, for example, but it will remain a book and can be put back in the shelf after its flight like any other book; a hairdryer may act as the west wind blowing the ship homewards, but it will still look like a hairdryer.

Size and shape become fluid. Free from all visible human characteristics, a tomato, held in the hand of an actor, need not in the world of object theatre be seen in the relative scale of big actor and small tomato. It can be as big as the sun or as small as an ant's brain. Nor does it have to stay as the sun or the ant's brain. It can become a clown's nose or can squash into bloody torture. A road digger can make a monster and so can a clothes peg.

The limits of reality are infinitely elastic in the hands of skilled animators. Much of this type of performance relies on visual effects, music, lighting and sounds more than on words, though a strong narrative drive often fuels the show.

It could happen like this ...

The lovers kiss on stage and swear eternal faithfulness. The book, apparently a perfectly ordinary book in a bookshelf of other books, is taken from the shelf by its animator. It flutters as a white dove with a blue ribbon round its neck above the lovers' heads. It hovers over the front rows of the audience. It doesn't speak but we hear it cheeping a romantic ballad as it swoops and dives. It is closer to the spirit of irony than its more habitual role as the spirit of peace. Puppets and objects are good at irony. They are already half way there, as the audience believes that they are being one thing and meaning another.

The practical side of this dove/book is the result of experiment in rehearsal and workshop. The covers look like a heavy, leather-bound volume when taken from the shelf because the actor is careful to angle the book spine-up so that gravity makes the cover lie smooth and firm. The weight is an illusion created by the actor's movement, while the covers are cut from the supple cream leather of an old skirt dyed brown on the outside and decorated with gold lettering. The 'pages' are silk and conceal the suggestion of a head and beak, and a blue ribbon 'bookmark' appears when the book is held upside-down with the covers/wings open wide. The whole can clip onto a rod which is used to make it flutter over the lovers and audience. The result is wry, comic and touching.

We see what we want to see – is it an old lady in a shawl or a young girl turning away from us? (The mouth of the old lady can be seen as the necklace of the girl.)

straight actors and puppeteers. They are often multilingual in the same way as a circus or an orchestra which includes many different nationalities united by the common language of movement or music. The free-form nature of the performance allows the audience to recognize its own experience of life in a way that is closer to listening to music than seeing a play. Themes such as Everyman's journey through the storm of life, a quest for some sort of grail or happiness, or escape and imprisonment may form a baseline for a plot that is more like a revue of different and internal aspects of our common humanity, rather than a definite story. Other plays with a strong narrative drive use the imaginative possibilities of object theatre to free them from the constraints of realism and allow them to enter a world where it is acceptable for walls to vanish

Themes

The stories of the most visual work tend to be open and mythic in content. They need to be simple as there may be few or no words. Companies include performers who are dancers, acrobats, musicians and improvisers as well as

It could happen like this ...

In the workshops of Au Cul du Loup, objects and music work together to create mysterious, comic or bizarre performance. Beautiful and extraordinary objects are made from materials which are more likely to have been sourced from the scrapyard or builders' merchant than the art shop. The maker/performers are welders, inventors, carpenters, singers, sculptors and actors who invent in the cheerful clutter of the workshop, kitchen, music room and barn. The components of the objects are not disguised. They look like the wood, metal and plastic they are. They are recognizable as ventilation ducts or ballcocks or wooden slats but also as sculptural abstract forms.

The forces that makes these objects work are nursery-simple – the natural urge of water to find its level, of air to fill a vacuum and of gravity to make things fall. Nothing extraordinary or complicated. The magic happens when the objects are moved and the gravity, air and water come into play through valves and twangers, reeds and percussion. The skilful and inventive players weave these objects and sounds into events as concrete as knights on horseback and as abstract as singing rolling spheres. Watching the mixture of dance, clowning and music with which the performers move the strangely beautiful objects creates an atmosphere that gives its audience the chance to recapture its delight in the beauty and funniness of our world.

For further information about Compagnie Au Cul du Loup, visit www.auculduloup.com

Objects from the workshops of Au Cul du Loup that will sing and perform with the natural movement of air, water and gravity.

and for an imaginary world to exist down the back of a sofa.

Of course, this is not to everyone's taste any more than is abstraction in painting or poetry. But it gives those who long for their eyes and hearts to be surprised a most intense experience. This all sounds serious stuff. But bouncing about just below the surface of any physical and visual work is the comedy of humans going about their lives with such solemn intent, and the anarchic and unstoppable power of laughter. The pratfalls and misunderstandings, and the visual humour of clowning which has entertained audiences for thousands and thousands of years, break through the surface of concentration and spirituality and connive with the audience in mutual understanding.

THE STARTING POINT

Companies that work with objects tend to have their own way of beginning their journey through rehearsals towards the performance. These will be discussed below.

An Object
For many, the first step is to choose one particular object or piece of scenery that becomes central to the path the story will follow. Imagine it to be an outsize bed; a bed that is big enough to form most of the stage area, with pillows the size of a donkey. Someone, probably the instigator of the project, will have had an idea of a bed as the heart of the story, and perhaps a picture in their mind of the hero and heroine lying small and asleep in the middle of this great expanse of bed. The director talks to the designer. The designer suggests that the bed should be raked (which means that it will be built on a slant so that the head end is much higher than the foot), and that it should be covered with a huge patchwork quilt that will suggest the rural and rather old-fashioned ambience of the story. The designer then makes a small model of the bed.

The dramaturg and director see that:

- the difference in scale between the huge but realistic-looking bed, its giant-size pillows and the actors will stress the vulnerability of the couple in the story
- the bed must be able to be removed so that the whole story isn't ruled by its permanent presence

- the unsophisticated background to the drama is set in place by the design of the patchwork cover
- the rake makes the action on the bed more easily visible to the audience
- a wealth of possibility is created by the space under the bed, which is big enough for people to hide in
- the seams between the different colours of the quilt can conceal slits where hands, heads and bodies can appear through the bed.

The maker of the bed and its covers sees that:

- the framework of the bed must be strong and sturdy as the action will take place under and through it as well as on top of it
- it must be possible to dismantle and reassemble the frame for storage and touring
- the baseboard on which people sit and lie cannot be solid as actors have to appear through the slits in the quilt
- the bed must be filled in at the sides so that the audience does not see the actors underneath it
- there must be an entrance for the actors, which is out of sight of the audience, to the area under the bed.

The composer sees that:

- the rural setting of the piece can be present in the folk-feeling of the music
- the lovers may have a theme which follows them through the journey of their affair
- the comic or sinister potential of the characters appearing through the entrances in the quilt can be enhanced by the feeling of the music.

*Dwarfed
by the
huge bed.*

*Hands
appearing
through the
bed.*

It becomes apparent during rehearsal that:

- the bed's baseboard must be made of a complex system of slats so that actors on top of the bed can stand, sit or lie on top of the bed, while others can come up through this apparently solid surface
- any bars or supports under the bed must be padded to mitigate accidents as actors squat or kneel under the bed waiting to appear through the quilt
- the area in the baseboard not covered with slats of wood must be covered in some way or the quilt will sink through the gaps
- the best way to do this is to cover the baseboard of slats with tight-stretched Lycra. Slits could be cut in the Lycra, which would stretch enough to allow a body to pass through but close up again afterwards to cover the gaps
- the quilt would have to be attached to the bed frame in places so that it did not slip about during the course of the action.

The lighting designer sees that:

- warm lighting without too much strong colour will best show the colours of the huge quilt
- careful experiment will be needed to ensure that the actors appearing through the bed will be seen clearly and not blend in a mess of colour with each other or the bright quilt colours
- there is a possibility for an effect that will bleach out the colours of the quilt and so produce a romantic or melancholy picture of the two lovers asleep on their floating moonlit bed.

Because an object like this becomes so integral to the action of the play it is important that it is ready, or at least that a rough-made mock-up is ready, for rehearsals. It is often better to have a mock-up than to rehearse with the real thing, as ideas will come during the course of rehearsal that will cause additions or alterations to be made to the bed.

A Story

For some, the first step is a story which is open enough to allow for a new method of interpretation. There is an archaeological site near the company base. Objects have been discovered, one of which is a tessera, a small ceramic tile divided in two parts found in two different homes on the site. This fact, combined with the old story of the divided talisman that inspires its two owners to try to reunite its parts, instigates the work.

The dramaturg and director see that:

- the battle between the Celts and the Romans which happened at the site gives a chance for dramatic action
- the tessera could have been divided by two friends or lovers before the battle as a token of undying love or friendship
- an epic series of events where the presence of the tessera is the catalyst could pull the story through the centuries
- the work could be about the journey to unite the two halves as one half travels through the centuries and the other remains at the site
- the possibilities of characters played by the same actors throughout the piece will be enhanced by the presence of the tessera in each scene
- there is room for the true story of the architectural site to be told through a series of imagined events.

The designer sees that:

- the tessera, though a small, realistic object in itself, should contain within it the possibility of change
- there might be an advantage to the story if one half of the tessera remains unchanged in size and shape while the other half has magic properties that allow it to transform
- in order to make this clear to the audience the tessera must be very distinctive in colour, pattern and shape so that it will always be recognizable in its transformations, be they jug, dress or boat.

The composer/sound designer sees that:

- due to a lack of actors the battle should be created with sound
- the tessera must have its own sound
- the transformations of the tessera must be accompanied by their own sounds to make the magic in what is happening to it clear to the audience.

The lighting designer sees that:

- the battle can be created with light and shadow
- the atmosphere of the journey through centuries and countries can be created through the lighting changes
- the transformations of the tessera should have their own special spotlight which pinpoints the change to the audience.

The production manager sees that:

- the story originating in the archaeological site might prove a springboard for funding
- epic journeys can be expensive to stage and a way must be found to create the array of people and places without employing a huge cast
- like an iceberg, the project will have more creative artists working out of sight than are visible in the light of the stage

Objects found by archaeologists at the site and used for design stimuli.

Design for both costumes for the actress and puppet of the same character.

31

The puppet.

- a careful schedule must be made if the outcome is to be achieved within the time and budget.

It becomes apparent through rehearsal that:

- the transformations of the half-tessera could be clarified by a large projected image of the two halves shown together but not conjoined
- the final joining of the tessera will be the climax of the show
- the actor who carries the tessera through the ages should play all the different people who inherit it
- there should be some echo in the design of set, costume and objects, which reminds the audience of the place and origin of the tessera.

A Company

The instigation of a company may arise from a combination of talents, skills and interest that are primed to explode in a group who want to work together. Maybe a musician, a writer/director, a designer/maker, a puppeteer and a straight actor feel a connection in their ideas and aspirations. They want to assemble a company and invent a performance that gives them all the opportunity to explore that connection. One place to combine their skills and ideas is within the loose and inventive circle of a performance, which uses objects and puppets, music, text and visual effects.

The director/writer sees the opportunity to:

- tell an old story in a new way
- write for a group who will use his or her work to its best advantage
- gather all the assembled talents of the company into an exciting, coherent performance
- bring together many creative minds working on one project under strong management with coherent direction.

The musician sees the opportunity to:

- invent work that uses the talents of the other company members as inspiration
- develop work during the rehearsal process, and not alone before or after the process
- use ideas for a soundscape composed of the noises the objects make.

The designer/maker sees the opportunity to:

- try combinations of ideas where the collaborative work in rehearsal replaces much of the solo work in the studio

- create work where the technical side of the design is developed at the same time as the artistic invention
- use his or her skill as a prop designer and maker to inspire and be inspired by the skills of the performers.

The puppeteer sees the opportunity to:

- break away from more traditional puppetry and experiment with other performance skills
- use his or her powers of invention in a more collaborative way
- become a more visible performer whilst using his or her practised ability to animate objects.

The actor sees the opportunity to:

- develop the skill of object animation which will use his or her natural ability to move well
- work with a new company for a different audience
- place ideas concerning audience participation that he or she has always wanted to try out.

They all see that:

- they can create between them an interesting job with a congenial and exciting group that will give them the chance to play with their ideas

A rehearsal room where director, actors, musicians and designers all work together.

- they need a production manager and a stage manager to control the practical aspects of the invention
- they need funding.

They may not all see that:

- their ideas belong to the group and the project and do not remain their property and under their control once they have been let loose in rehearsal
- it will be emotionally difficult to throw away ideas that may have been produced through a lot of rehearsal time, and be good in themselves, but do not fit in with the project.

Funding

It might seem the wrong way round to be inspired to a great surge of energy and invention by something as prosaic as money, but it happens. It may be possible to fund a project if, perhaps, its content can support an exhibition about genetics or will employ a local community in its production. It is much more difficult to produce work without money than to invent ideas that will both satisfy a funder's criteria and the creative interests of a company.

Of course, there are as many different ways of starting up the machinery of creating a performance as there are performances and companies. But object theatre, perhaps because it tends to involve an unusual collection of skills, is likely to spring from collaboration and the exchange of ideas. It would be unusual for a completed and edited object theatre script to drop through the letterbox, or to arrive on the computer screen of an actor, a composer, a director or a designer, and for the rehearsals to create a direct enactment of the words. When a performer starts animating an object ideas develop and everyone

It could happen like this ...

The company are at the beginning of working together. The progress of the story they are working on is unsure, but there are some ideas that are set. The story will happen somewhere in Eastern Europe in the late 1930s or 1940s and it will concern the sort of incongruity that makes an innocent child become an armed soldier and a baby's pram to be full of dynamite. It will also involve the incongruous nature of true love and clowning existing in dark and tragic situations.

The set, costume and props will look as if they are a jumble of objects that could have been found in anyone's attic at that time. The objects will be used to tell the story as much as the actors and will be able to take on human or animal characteristics if necessary to the plot. There may not be many words but there will be music and the physical ability of the performers will be used to the full.

The prop store is raided for a pile of objects that look as if they belong to the period and hold within themselves a sort of emotional charge: a bunch of wildflowers with a single red rose in the middle; a violin case (does it hold a fiddle or a shotgun or just music?); a puppet baby in a shawl. A rail of costumes of the era stands at the side of the rehearsal room with a table of hats and bags and accessories.

The actors begin to play at games and improvisations, helping themselves from the piles of costumes and objects as they build their characters. The performance will grow through the weeks of rehearsals from these early beginnings.

For further information about the Fred is Dead company of St Mary's University College, Twickenham, visit www.smuc.ac.uk/Courses/Undergraduate/index/

begins to play with possibilities. The difficulty comes in gathering and refining the ideas, chucking out the ones that are inappropriate and binding the good ones together into a play.

It is rare for this type of work to be written, then cast and rehearsed; a more likely situation is for a group of performers to be assembled as a bunch of different but compatible talents, a rough idea of the sort of performance expounded, and experimental sessions in the workroom set in action. The differing strengths of the company – actors, puppeteers, dancers, designers and musicians – will soon become clear; indeed, the group may have been chosen with a particular variety of skills in mind. The work of the director is to balance and manage the possibilities and blend them into a homogenous performance.

Everyone is an inventor both in the rehearsal room and in the audience. Physical and visual information in such performance demands a particular sort of involvement from members of the audience. They must agree to believe that the objects and sights they see, whether prosaic or bizarre, do actually possess the meaning the actors give them, and suspend their disbelief to a greater extent than they do in more conventional performance.

Actors from the Fred is Dead company of St Mary's University College Twickenham work with objects and costumes in an improvisation rehearsal.

3. VISUAL EFFECTS, SHADOWS, SCALE AND SOUND

Some of the most abstract theatre gets its initial stimulus from an idea that is visual, rather than narrative and concrete, and uses sets and objects that transform to help create the performance. A more down-to-earth background may be put in place behind the picture, but the primary impetus will have been a flight of fancy that lit a longing in the practitioners to make it leap onto the stage. These ideas are easy to talk about in a rehearsal room with a group of like-minded fellow workers. They tend, however, to be difficult to pin down to the black and white words on a page. It can sound a bit weak to say, 'We just wanted to see what would happen.' or 'We thought it would be interesting if …', but that is often the truth of the matter. The strong and daring working groups bonded by this longing for experiment form the strength of company-devised work.

We are used to narrative-free drama in painting, circus, dance and music, but many people in the audience feel a need to identify with the characters onstage. Actors may want to build a recognizable character to flesh out a performance which may be intensely physical and spiritual or funny but not rooted in any concrete reality. This can lead the companies who perform such visually exciting work to create some sort of story which will link the dreamlike, surreal or comic life on stage to a more earthy reality. The idea may have been figures, mythical, battered and beautiful, blown by a gigantic and roaring gale, fighting, leaning and tumbling in the tumultuous current of air; tattered strips of cloth, hair streaming parallel to the ground in the music and light of the storm. The story, which roots this wild and splendid extravagance into our grasp, is about a group of humans desperately trying to preserve their way of life from destruction.

Much of this work, labelled experimental and cutting edge, not by its makers but by academics and critics, relies on a basis of good old theatrical trickery. These traditional effects have reappeared on today's stage strengthened by the wonderful lighting, sound and projection that are now available to inventors of theatre.

The transformations of objects are as likely to be funny as breathtakingly beautiful. The bizarre juxtaposition of an everyday object adopting a new character and being so real and believable in its new identity makes people laugh. It is so unexpected to see a loaf of bread starting to talk or a snowstorm erupting from a handbag.

A cut-out boat sails through a sea of theatrical trickery. Photo: Alistair Milne

VISUAL EFFECTS

The traditional low-tech theatrical tricks of starcloths, gauzes and wind, shadows and snow have kept their magic. These effects are an integral part of many object and visual theatre productions and have to be considered under the same umbrella; they behave like objects, surprising and delighting the audience in much the same way. They have been joined by new, more complex effects that are supported by exciting innovations. The use of projection and computerized operation makes it possible for clouds to scud across a cyclorama or the audience to watch giant pictures being drawn by an invisible hand. Effects of lighting, sound and engineering offer designers and directors more opportunities in the way they present the play to the audience. These effects can all be bought, but many of them have always existed in more simple form and it can be possible to tell the same story with low-budget trickery.

Snow

A big bag of theatrical snow is cheap to buy and comes fireproofed and ready to drop. You can sweep it up and use it again a few times. Torn-up paper will make snowflakes if the budget is tight; the paper from a paper shredder is already cut into strips. Printer paper is fine; tissue paper a bit too insubstantial. Check the fire regulations in your venue. It is a simple matter to rig up a method of getting 'the snow' to drop on cue even if you cannot get someone high enough above the stage to be out of the

Figures in a projected jungle photo. Photo: Alistair Milne

sight lines. Leaves, petals, glitter and so on will work in the same way. The higher the start of the drop from the stage, the wider the spread of snow. It can be encouraged to swirl by wind from the wings.

Wind

Wind machines are expensive and in a small venue will create a considerable amount of background noise. This will not matter if the wind is supposed to be part of a howling storm, but is not so good if a gentle breeze is required. Any large piece of flat wood or cardboard will work as a giant, silent fan in the wings, but the best method to displace a lot of air is by using a thick sheet of polystyrene or foam insulation board; use the biggest sheet whose weight you can handle and that you can wave without it cracking under the strain.

Smoke, Mist and Haze

There is not much you can do to make smoke or haze without a theatre machine made for the purpose. It is a worthwhile expense for a small company as it makes so many lighting and other visual effects appear even more magical. A smoke machine puffs out directional jets of steam and most make a noise when they do so. A hazer fills a space silently with mist that only shows when the light is on it.

Starcloths

You can bodge up a starcloth with any dark, lightproof piece of cloth punched with holes to let the light from behind shine through. The holes do not have to be star-shaped – just round holes not less than 2cm in diameter. Fairy lights can be used to magical effect on a black background if the flex is painted black to match.

Lighting

Lighting in theatre production is a potent force. It can create mood and time, weather and place, set, reality and fantasy. It can direct the attention of members of the audience to a particular happening while making them ignore another. It can flood an area with clear daylight or create a pool of candle glow in the middle of a huge stage. It can frame an event with the accuracy of a camera lens.

Many of the objects and puppets used onstage are small; much smaller than their animators. It can be important to direct bright light to these objects and allow the animators to fade, not from view, but from the conscious attention of the audience. Light, and any movement in light, will draw the eye. Our eyes instinctively focus on the brightly lit spot; it requires a more conscious effort to search the shadows. Lighting designers have a delicate and detailed role to play in puppet and object performance. Sometimes they will be lighting a moment that, though tiny in size, has a huge importance to the narrative onstage. At other times, they will be lighting giants in dark forests or a conversation between a thumb-high figure and a human. There may be times when there is simply not enough money to use proper stage lighting equipment. If you are having to make do with non-theatrical equipment such as builders' halogen lamps or school overhead projectors, keep it simple and make sure the audience can see what they are supposed to; if necessary, adapt the idea to fit with the available lighting.

Projection

Projection produces magical effects. The Internet is full of images that can be projected into theatres; some are in copyright but many are free. The best projectors are expensive, but exciting effects can be produced with an ordinary data projector or even a carousel slide projector. If the projector does not have a high lumen output, the surrounding lighting will have to be lowered for the picture to show.

Gobos are circular stencils that allow you to create a shape with light, by being placed between the projector's lamp and the lens. Imagine a light shining through a stencil with a cross cut out of it; the image of the cross will appear where the light lands. If you create your own gobo for a stage light you must use something that will not burn or buckle in intense heat, for example printer's lithoplate. You can, however, make a screen with a design that will stand at a safe distance in front of the light and project the image in this way.

All these effects can work in a small venue but they take time to get right. The most frequent cause of failure is leaving too short a time to rehearse the technical aspects of the show.

SHADOWS AND SHADOW PUPPETS

Shadows belong to the time when our imaginations were most fertile. They come from the childhood evenings of stories and bedtime and stay with us through adult walks lit by street-lights. They live on the beach in the tall, thin horizontal figure attached to your feet. If you squat, the tall, thin figure lying on the sand shrinks to an undefined lump. If you jump, the shadow detaches and rejoins you when land. Throw a towel into the middle of it and the towel will vanish. Splay the hand above the head and the shadow loses its human form. A cloud comes and it vanishes.

The strength of this genre lies in the human ability to recognize silhouette. How often have you recognized the back view of someone you love when the detail is flattened by bright sun-light? Why, before photographs were available, did people have their likenesses taken as silhouettes in profile? How can the pattern and relative spacing of the common features and bones in a human face be so subtle and individual yet recognizable? We are all in-stinctively able to decode silhouette but are mostly unaware of the subtlety and thorough-ness of our skill.

The Puppets

The instant picture that slides into most minds when shadow puppets are mentioned is the stylized Eastern silhouettes that belong in tra-ditional performance. The puppets that play out these stories are complex and beautiful works of art, and the shadows they cast on the screen reflect the years of traditional skill that

It could happen like this ...

2002 and the invasion of Iraq and everyone is thinking about oil. The puppeteer/ inventors of Indefinite Articles think about oil, too. They fill a rectangular glass baking dish with it, set it on an overhead projector and switch on the light. A rich and strange effect appears on the screen, which reacts to any change in the baking dish: colour the oil pink and it is sunset; swirl in blue and the night sky appears; sweep a paintbrush handle across it and a comet flies through space; dab it with a paintbrush handle and with each dab a new star shines on the screen. Oil makes the background to the play as well as the politics.

The play is *The Magic Lamp*, a retelling of Scheherazade's story of Aladdin. The characters and objects are shadows and silhouettes. The props that help tell the story, including the wonderful magic lamp, appear on the screen as an image of the cardboard shapes placed on the projectors' platform. The Genie is another swirling effect made by the oil. Jewels appear and disappear in a mysterious cave as drops of coloured paint are added to the dish of oil and disperse slowly in the liquid.

The scope of the story could use a large cast and the entire range of technical effects in the best-equipped theatre. But this is different. For a start, it is shadow puppetry in the round. There is an overhead projector on each side of the screen. The screen is thin nylon, only just opaque. The audience sits each side of it and the image from both projectors can be seen from both sides. There is only one actor, who is sometimes one side of the screen and sometimes the other; you may see him or you may see his shadow. There is another performer who makes the pictures that send their shadows onto the screen. The story is made for each performance with the arrangements of paper cut-outs, coloured liquid and oil on the platforms of the overhead projectors, and the light which sends single or overlapping shadows onto the screen.

For more Indefinite Articles, email tipladysg@aol.com

have gone into perfecting them and educating the audience to understand their subtleties. Think more into your own experience and the children's game of making the hand's shadow on the wall into a rabbit, or of the lampshade's pattern projecting silhouettes as the light passes through. Think of the overlapping shadows when the light from two streetlights crosses.

Shadows have a particular magic. They are experts in the art of transformation. Hold a shadow puppet close to the screen and the picture it throws will be crisp and clear; move it away and the picture grows and blurs. A simple shadow puppet, such as a cardboard cut-out of a man on a stick, is capable of many actions, all of which will be clearer if we see him in profile. There is a more distinctive silhouette to the profile than to the straight-ahead face, plus we

can see the eye. The profile of the nose helps the audience to follow the puppet's focus. Providing him with a moving joint worked by a rod will give him a much more active life. Images and colours can be overlaid. Having several different light sources adds to the possibilities. It is no problem for the shadow whale to swallow Jonah; the whale's shadow will eat him with ease.

Shadow puppetry is not confined to the creation of characters. The treadmill wheel turning on the prison set or the gaunt winter trees on the ridge of a hill can use the same principle to set time and place as to set character onstage.

The Screen
Taut-stretched cotton makes a good screen. So

Shadows tell stories with simple clarity.

does Lycra. Any marks, dirt or pattern in the weave that prevent the light passing evenly through the cloth will be thrown into sharp focus and exaggerated by the light, so the screen, unlike most theatre props and scenery, has to be clean and look clean in order to present a sharp shadow. Shadows are bigger when they are near the light source and smaller when further away. The shadows don't have to be grey or black; the picture can be coloured provided the objects casting the shadows are made of a material that the light can pass through.

Light

Creating the right light for shadow play is a matter of angles and precision and juggling the available space with the position of the actor or object combined with the brightness of the light. None of the careful work on character and story, making the puppets and learning to animate them will be of any use to the audience unless the lighting and the positions of animators and puppets are right. It can take a long time to get this right, and it is not always possible to experiment in the rehearsal room with the right lighting conditions and the right space. There will need to be enough rehearsal time in performance conditions to make sure every moment throws good shadows onto the screen.

Once you start to play with a light source, a blank wall, some paper and scissors, the possibilities start unfolding. Look at the way light changes when it passes through water, bubble wrap or coloured cellophane, and the variations in the shadow of a two-dimensional object when seen from different angles. The magic of changing shadows is simple physics but which holds all the storytelling possibilities of scale and surprise.

SCALE

The question of scale in relation to puppets and objects is complex and difficult to pin down. It is usual for the features of puppets to be exaggerated; for noses, eyes and hands to be larger in relation to the face and body than is usual in humans. This would seem the most likely way for these tiny faces to be expressive at a distance. But then you see a puppet with hardly any features but which can convey a wealth of emotion with a tilt of the chin or a turn of the head and the theory falls apart. The only rule seems to be 'if it works, use it', which is not particularly useful to the novice puppet maker. Experiment seems more useful than any rulebook.

The great advantage of the invisible puppeteer is that the scale of the puppets and objects is infinitely variable. The audience has no real people to create the comparison that nails down a perception of the actual size of the puppets. A 20cm (8in) high man will walk through a 30cm (12in) high archway into a wood of ancient 50cm (2in) high oak trees. Provided that the space in which this little forest is contained is defined and separate from the audience's space, there will be no clue as to the trees' real-life size; there will be a man, an archway and a tree and no argument about it. If someone should place a real chair behind the archway the illusion will be destroyed, unless the audience is so involved that it translates this as a giant's chair. When the audience cannot see the animator at all, the puppet appears in its own world. This gives opportunities to create an environment scaled to the puppets' size. A pint-sized Goliath will appear huge to a teacup-sized David. Mountains and deserts, crowds and horses in the surrounding landscape will all reinforce the reality of the scale.

It could happen like this ...

The Sultan's Elephant

For four days in spring 2006 the centre of London was transformed. The Sultan's Elephant, on his travels round countries and cities, came to England. The elephant was as tall as a two-storey house. It watered the window boxes upstairs with its trunk. It trumpeted and waved its magnificent leather ears. Benign, a little mischievous and absolutely huge, it was attended, not only by its animator and its band, but also by an awestruck and delighted crowd. The workmanship was wonderful and the spirit delightful and free. There was, however, more to the elephant than met the eye. The pace of its movement was in direct ratio to its size. It seemed to move fast because it was so huge, but in fact the rhythm of its footsteps, and its gravitas, slowed the pace of its audience. A fragile ribbon maintained a clear surround for it to move in and kept the audience safely clear of its mechanics, and was all that was needed to keep even the most unruly child at a safe distance. The scale was not only apparent in size, but in this alteration of pace, and in the rolling length of the laughter when it sprayed the audience with mist from its trunk. It met on its journey a girl as tall as a lamp post, who knelt down to allow the children in the crowd to ride on her extended forearms. The change to the habitual rhythm of the spectators was irresistible and subtle, but united the humans around it – most of them Londoners who live in such a hectic rush – in a spirit of calm friendliness and play.

For further information about Royal de Luxe and the Sultan's Elephant, visit
www.thesultanselephant.com/about/royaldeluxe.php

A more complex distortion of scale occurs when objects made to different scales appear in the same space and story. It might be difficult for the audience to make this adjustment of perception if either of the objects were real. An army is presented by troops of grey-painted eggs that march together in their segmented egg tray to the beat of a drum. The lone soldier who watches their approach must be made in a larger scale unless the audience is very small and close; an egg-sized lone soldier will not be read clearly from a distance. But he can be taller than an egg. Not as tall as a real man, perhaps ten times the height of the eggs and the illusion will hold; the audience will assess the size of the army with the abstract understanding they use when they follow the suggestions of music or poetry.

Should a mistake happen onstage, the sight of a real human hand appearing would jerk the audience out of its involvement. For this reason, a hand on the end of a stick, sometimes equipped with a grab action, may be kept to pick up a dropped hat or to nudge a misplaced chair into place. The audience will enjoy the joke as part of the performance and return to the action with an uninterrupted viewpoint. It is always astonishing to see marionettes backstage after the performance; audience eyes and brains will have reconstructed the figures to a human scale and it will seem almost impossible that the hero, in his offstage reality, is the size of a little child. When the hands or even the whole body of the

Royal de Luxe's street theatre on a grand scale: LEFT: *the elephant* BELOW: *the huge girl. Photos: David Bieda*

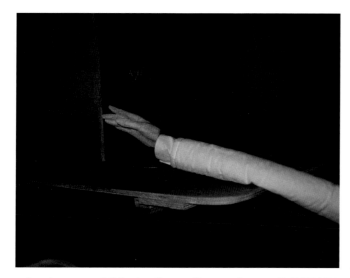

The hand that appears from the wings to collect a dropped prop.

animator are visible to the audience these games with scale are not possible. This does not make the characters seem less real; the eyes of the viewers translate the message differently, with the result that they edit and rationalize the visual world on stage so that they believe in it.

Scale does not only relate to the size of the puppets and objects. There is a rhythm in movement that relates to the size but it is not quite the same in the puppet/object world as it is in real life. A mosquito moves very quickly. It is also very small. A puppet mosquito would probably be larger than life and the puppet man it bites smaller than a real one, with his reactions being a little slower. The puppet mosquito cannot move as fast as a real one or the audience would not be able to register its flight. The audience has to have time to locate it, follow its passage and see the man try to swat it. It is possible to convey the feeling of speed with the fast, high-whining *DZZDZ* of the insect while it buzzes about without speeding up the actual movement.

SOUND

The use of a soundscape of music and effects replaces all sorts of explanation in much object and visual theatre production. There are two basic ways of providing the near-continuous soundtrack that is likely to accompany this genre of work. One is to pre-record the whole soundtrack of the piece, in which case the work is performed to synchronize with the sound. Should something go wrong, the sound must be stopped or the performers find some way of getting back on track. The other way is for the sound engineer to have a creative role in the performance and to phase and phrase the sound cues according to the progress of the performance onstage. The sound cues can be timed through a sensitive understanding of the level of emotion and energy onstage; the sound engineer can overlap cues, alter the volume and generally make the sound behave as a performer within the context of the piece rather than as an adjunct or replacement for onstage voice. He or she performs as a musician as well as an engineer.

It could happen like this ...

A strange object swings gently in the air and the light. There is no scenery surrounding it. It is a platform made of a grid of metal poles. Nothing tells us, the audience, that the three sleeping people in ordinary clothes are shipwrecked survivors but the sounds of gently slapping waves, three-second-long ghost moments of dance band music, a distant foghorn and seagull and a just-audible background of noises we associate with the sea. In five seconds and with no words, the place, the weather, the people and the mood have been explained to us.

They are explained because a musician has squatted on a harbour wall early one foggy morning with a microphone and made a collection of sounds to take back to his studio. There he chooses a collage of these sounds interspersed with the music he composes to allow us to share the mood of the actors onstage. The musician and the sound operator work together in rehearsal to decide the volume and the way the sounds will overlap. The sound operator becomes an invisible performer as he blends the soundscape with the action throughout each performance. This gives him a more creative part in the performance as volume, timing and possible combinations of sounds can support the mood of the action on stage.

For further information about Ockham's Razor, contact ockhamsrazor@gawab.com

A platform rocks in the air ... A movement from Arc *by Ockham's Razor. Photo: Marion Kingwill*

The designer creating the sound will have spent time in rehearsal getting close to the development of the action onstage. He or she may write or choose music, but may also create an environment of sounds, a sense of place, which has more power than any visual message to establish an onstage world for the audience.

4. SCRIPTS AND STIMULI

SCRIPTS

Choosing Scripts and Stories

A script might be used as a starting point for improvisation, but any script to be followed word for word would have been created through the process of another object-based performance. The form of the script must allow for an interpretation in which the visual side is as important as the words the actors speak. It is a relatively new genre in its present form and so the published scripts are of productions created by companies that perform this very visual sort of work. There is, however, a history of puppet performance which has a long back catalogue of plays, masques and mystery plays in which the spectacle and physicality of the performers took a major part in the show.

All sorts of plays and characters have been and are played by puppets, but the ones that people choose over and over again live in mythic, epic, fantastical or comical worlds. Faust, Red Riding Hood and the Minotaur all settle confidently on a puppet stage. Moses and every one of the children of Israel could pass through the watery corridor of the Red Sea in a blink of the eye. An actor playing Everyman can share the stage with a puppet playing an Angel; they come from different species and it seems natural that they should be played in different styles. Opera, which always demands from the audience a belief and an emotional engagement with an extraordinary world, works well when puppets act while the singers sing.

It is difficult to find the reason why some scripts work with puppets and others do not. It seems to have something to do with a certain clarity in the emotions. Puppets and objects, a step a way from their animators, divulge an uncluttered message. Their souls may be tormented and their natures complex, but they have to send a pure, unfuzzy message of their emotional turmoil or the audience will not interpret their feelings with certainty. The triangle of object, animator and audience needs to be clear or the audience loses confidence in its interpretation of the action and disengages its commitment to the work.

Puppets in the right hands have an extraordinary ability to slip under people's guard, bypass the intellect and engage the emotions in the most direct and unexpected manner. They have attributes that humans have always longed for and actors have to be given complicated technical help to appear to achieve. Puppets can fly and change their shape. Their bodies can be light and transparent or seem as dense as lead. They can be high as a house or the size of a thumb. And they can speak in any voice that is given them. What actor would not long to have all those skills at the top of their CV?

There may be other reasons, financial, political or practical, why it is not possible or advisable to use human actors to perform a play. In the skilled hand of a single performer a crowd can appear on a shoebox and pack up in it after the show. They cost less to clothe than actors and use less fabric. Their make-up does not have to be retouched for every show and, unlike their animators, they don't have difficult mothers or lovers or children with

---

It could happen like this ...

Rudi (as Fischer) and his girlfriend Sylvia (as Organ Grinder) play puppeteers who use traditional Jumping Jack puppets as a means to tell the story of a tragic loss of life during World War One. They are conscious that, as manipulators of the puppets, their roles symbolize those of ruthless political leaders.

Organ Grinder: Be happy with your life!
Fischer: Stop, Organ Grinder. Be quiet now. Your voice sounds like a creaking coffin. The song smells like a grave, so warm and earthy.
Grinder: Be happy with your life!
Fischer: I am Lieutenant Fischer! I have walked this path for years. I am only 25 and already I have lost one war. I have buried 57 of my soldiers near Boronesch. Before, they sang. After, their silence was deafening.
(Rudi pulls the strings of the Boxer Jumping Jack and then all the others in turn ...)
Fischer: A boxer with his thick fists cries, 'I am boxing, I am boxing.' A fat man with a party badge on his collar struts like a master. And who is that behind him? A general in his stupid uniform shouting back his orders. A Doctor Faust in his white coat and black mirrors, but he does not cry and he does not shout.

Excerpt from Bright Angel written by Chris Baldwin and Bernd Kessler. For further information, visit www.chrisbaldwin.org and www.brandenburgertheater.de

Rudi and his girlfriend Sylvia tell a tragic and political story.
Photo: Chris Baldwin

---

mumps. Puppets have been used to tell the politically dissident stories that might have caused a real actor or writer to be thrown into prison or sent off to bleak Siberia. And they have always been able to speak for the underdog. It would take a very brave or very stupid dictator to risk his dignity and credibility by arresting a bundle of sticks and rags.

Puppets are not introspective. This is not to say that the content of that long and serious speech by the puppet could not be shared with the audience, just that the method of delivery could not be so naturalistic and true to life. A more obviously theatrical method of delivery, possibly one which put an ironic or satirical slant on the content, might enable a puppet to underscore and illustrate the complications of the thoughts behind the words.

When an actor plays a role, the character he creates is a combination of his own character and that of the role he is performing; he is stuck with the person his parents made him and must make of it what he will. He remains, always, as the root of the characterization. The puppet has a much more varied family tree. His 'parents' are not the only material he is made from, but also the designer and the maker, the scriptwriter, the animator and the director. And he can't make of the role what he will; he has to make of it what they all will.

SCRIPTS FOR CHILDREN

Young children are surrounded by new and unfamiliar happenings every day of their lives. They tend to be much better than most adults at accepting the unknown and unexpected. An adult thinks nothing of switching on a light; they touch a switch and the light goes on. They may know or not know how electricity passes through the wires to work the magic, but they have done it a thousand times. The child presses the light switch and the light goes on; he presses it again and it goes off. And on. And off. And on. And off. Rules appear at the apparent whim of adults; why does pudding happen at the end of a meal and not the beginning? Why does mud count as dirty and sand count as clean? It takes time to sort out connections, reasons, cause and effect. And it takes time for young children to sort out the events onstage.

Scripts for young children need to allow for this exploration. The story must be simple and straightforward enough for the child to decode. This doesn't mean sweet and undemanding. It is more a case of getting to the heart of the matter and presenting it with clarity and truth, as well as respect for the child's interest and development.

Pace and Understanding

Humans learn language by hearing it and trying to use it. An adult may have heard the combination of words that make up a specific phrase thousands of times with many variations of pitch and accent; a five-year-old in the audience may be hearing it for the first time. Think of the phrase 'Get on with it!' Imagine what on earth you'd make of that phrase if you were at the beginning of learning English. It is complex. And odd. And however hard you try to translate it into its separate components, it remains pretty impenetrable. Its meaning depends on its place in the story, the way it is spoken, the volume, the pace and the gesture that accompanies the sound. Young children don't bother to do anything as long-winded and inefficient as a laborious translation; if the context is clear they will gather the phrase and its intention together as a chunk and absorb its meaning. If the plot is developed at speed with

49

consistently complicated language they will not be able to follow it.

The pace at which a production can proceed must be appropriate to the understanding of all the audience, even the youngest. It could seem impossible to balance this see-saw without boring the socks off those with more experience and setting off the shuffling restlessness that strikes fear in an actor's soul. This apparent dichotomy is solved by the wonderful editing skills of these little children; they make an instant selection of the words and actions appropriate to their understanding and ignore the rest. The playwright's skill comes in producing enough complexity to keep all these brains alert and engaged to the limit, or at best slightly beyond their usual limit, whilst making the broader plot line accessible to the less experienced playgoer.

Commissioning a Script

It is common, in the world of puppet, object and the more visual kinds of theatre, that the writer of the script will also be the director of the production, or the designer and possibly the maker of the company. Or all three and more. This doubling up of jobs may be fostered by the funding situation, which may not provide for the salaries of many different creative artists. Or it may be the result of the necessity to create a visual picture that is so closely allied to the story and style of the piece that it is not possible or practical for the jobs to be separate.

The idea may grow slowly, with the physical characteristics of the characters, the set, the costumes and sound growing together in the mind of the instigator of the work. This artist/craftsman may not actually be a writer, but the vision will grow until it is formed enough to be laid before a writer to carve into

a play. The instigator of the project will look for a writer or dramaturg who can understand and create a play that will keep the puppets, objects and visual effects afloat, and enable them to communicate the story to the audience.

Most writers would prefer to start with the minimum of information, rather than a detailed breakdown of the imaginings of the instigator. The story, or the book if it is an adaptation, and some knowledge of the style and length of the proposed work, is enough to begin the project. Artists who can create to the order of someone else's mind are rare, and everyone's best work comes from their own heart and experience. Many discussions during the creation of the script, particularly when a writer is used to his or her words pouring out of human mouths, will be needed before the words, and so many fewer words, can pour as naturally and informatively from puppets.

Because the work relies so much on visual effect to trick the audience into losing its preconceptions of reality, the writer cannot afford to give the audience long speeches or explanations that encourage a more literal expectation of human behaviour; these writers tread a tightrope line between keeping the word count low and saying enough to give the work depth and scope.

The dramatic possibilities expand when actors and puppets perform together. The subtlety and vulnerability of the human body and mind, stuck in the shape nature gave it, can enjoy a wonderful new freedom when it begins to perform with a puppet as its co-star. The two together, as an odd but equal partnership, can work as a whole that is greater than the sum of its parts. Frankness and directness are demanded of the actor when confronted by a puppet onstage. The puppet will have the audi-

It could happen like this ...

A request to the writer for an idea for a situation that would involve humans speaking in their everyday world, and their puppet versions singing what they felt in their hearts, instigated this response:

William and Liz aspire to be their glamorous alter egos, Puppet William and Puppet Liz. Puppet William and Puppet Liz do not speak but sing and make actions. William and Liz are unaware that their actions in the real world move a forest of rods that animate their alter egos. They reach for a mug of coffee in the real world of their office and their puppet alter ego above them is animated by the same gesture to raise a glass of champagne to their glamorous puppet companion.

William gets a date with Liz and Liz with William, but are they dating their fantasies (the puppets) or are the puppets the way they see each other?

There is also a BIG BOSS – just a head – perhaps a shadow puppet or part of the set. According to where the head is positioned, the audience sees just an eye, or a mouth or a bald head like a hill.

Incidents/scenes might be work, shopping, the date.

Sample dialogue:

William: Someone somewhere is living my life, only they are living it better, with better stuff among better people. The only thing is I can't see them but of course I know they are there. I can hear them singing –

(Puppet William sings a self-satisfied song as Human William tries to catch him.)

Excerpt from Twice Upon a Time *by Tony Bicât*

---

ence on its side as surely as a child or an animal would in the same circumstances. In order to hitch onto this wave of goodwill, the actor must manage to tap into the audience's confident belief in the puppet.

Research and Development

The research and development period (R&D) and the actual rehearsals for performance rarely take place as one continuous process. It is an expensive business to fund, as there would be so many people, actors, designers, writers, directors and technicians being paid over such a long time. It is good for the project to have time to settle and a time when the writer or dramaturg can shape the script to encompass the new ideas that emerge during the research period. A likely pattern is for periods of R&D to be separated by periods when most of the company is employed on other projects.

STIMULI

Stimuli for Object Theatre

The subject matter of object theatre work is more likely to come from an idea than from a script. Most such work is devised and written through the R&D period. Often the stimuli may come from several sources. You could pick a list of actual objects (a tin bath), people (Lewis Carroll), an emotional abstract (loss), poems ('The Ancient Mariner'), particular skills

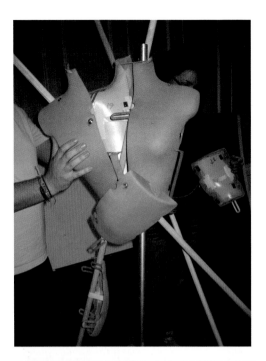

The dressmaker's dummy, fitted with magnetic joints for student actors of St Mary's University College to explore the subject of injury in a workshop with Josephine Machon.

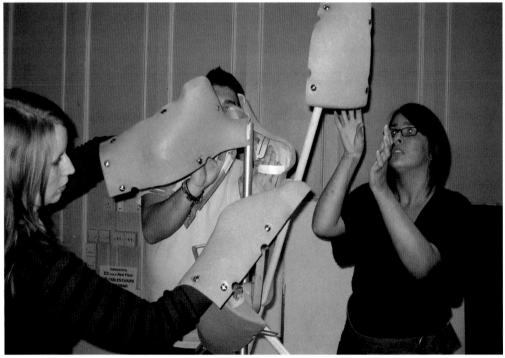

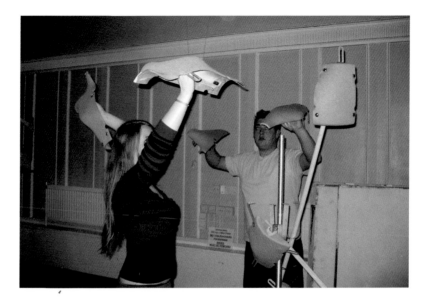

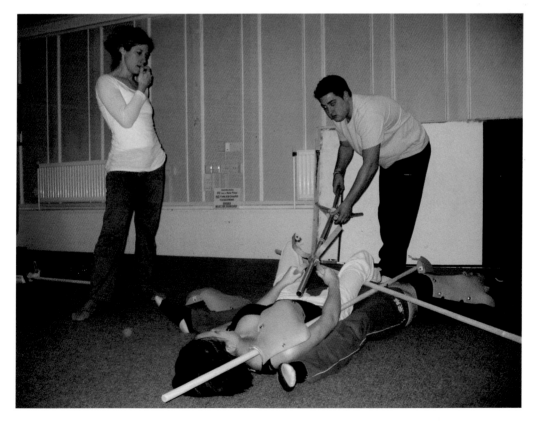

within the company (a cellist, a conjuror and an aerialist), philosophical or scientific concepts (Archimedes' principle), social issues (slavery in the eighteenth century) and available funding (for young people to explore the roots of their community), or almost any story and come up with a starting point for development.

The fact that the idea inspires and excites the company is as important as the idea itself; it is the development of the idea that makes the performance.

Scattering Ideas

It works to scatter ideas. Wonderful projects mulch in your head. Talk about thoughts for future projects, or if you find it difficult to talk, write about them and send them out into the world. It is easy to feel diffident about some of these thoughts that may seem too insubstantial to communicate, but none of them will come to anything unless you risk sharing them. Ideas grow when they are let out into the air; ideas you would like to play with, thoughts about stimuli that would interest other people who work in your field. If your ideas, perhaps as a writer, attract someone else's ideas as a designer, they might attract further ideas from a musician, a director, a choreographer, a producer and, with luck, a funder. Lots of these thoughts won't thrive,

but it is through this sort of chat that the new-stirring ideas for a project start to become real. It is also the way to form a team which can work with excitement together.

It all sounds a bit casual and amateur; a slapdash way to begin work on something that will absorb the driving creativity of a group through months or even years. But really, that is the way most projects of this nature begin their life, and often, at the start of their life, there is little more than chat and enthusiasm for them to grow on. There is no point in playing with this sort of work if you do not love it. People will give a huge amount of time and energy to a project they love and believe in, but the excitement and satisfaction there is in its growth are usually worth much more than its financial earning power. This means that directors, designers and technicians have to work in a different way, and this is true of the pre-production period as well as the rehearsal period. The budget will affect the amount of actors or animators who can be employed and this will, in turn, affect the amount of puppets and the complication of their manipulation.

A lot of these questions will have be thought about and discussed from the moment the project is conceived, but at some point definite decisions must be taken so that the work of constructing the puppets and working the rehearsals can begin.

5. PRODUCTION DECISIONS

EARLY DECISIONS

Once the script and content have been found, decisions can begin to be made about what sort of puppets will be used, whether the animators will be seen by the audience or hidden from view and whether the cast will consist of just puppets or a mixture of puppets and humans. If the humans are to be seen, will they be dressed in black with black gloves and hoods (sometimes a terrifying sight to a small child), or will the audience be able to see their hands and faces? Will the dialogue be live or will it be recorded? Which animator will work with which puppet, and will it be the same animator all the time or will puppets change hands at certain points in the performance?

Painted wooden shapes allow performers to use their own hands and faces. The priest in the middle is a wooden cut-out whose eyes can be moved.

Preparing for Take-Off

Decisions will need to be financial and practical as well as artistic. They may be made round the posh boardroom table or over a beer in the pub, but whether the budget is thousands of pounds or a frugal scraped-together chunk of the group's living expenses the facts under discussion will be remarkably similar. The longing to invent something that will really happen, the drive to create a performance, will have the same irresistible force. Pragmatic matters of venue, budget and timescale must be talked about even if no decision can be reached, along with the more exciting matters of subject and casting and assembling the creative team.

Decisions of a practical nature, such as allocating the budget, the number of performers, what skills they will need and who they will be, are addressed. It can be a most useful aid to the progress of these talks, particularly in the later stages, to have a cool and practical mind, such as that of a production manager, around to stop the ideas bouncing too far from the solid ground of possibility. Many of these decisions will be decided by the budget. Time for rehearsal means money to pay for rehearsal space and money to pay the performers and crew. If people are not being paid for their work, they need time for making the money that they must earn elsewhere to feed themselves and their children. But the urge to invent and perform is a resilient one and adverse circumstances won't stop those imbued with it from finding ways to make things happen.

Pre-Production Questions

Whatever the project, there are some basic questions to be answered:

- Who is your target audience?

- When do you plan to work on and perform the piece? How long is the expected run and how long is the rehearsal period? This decision has to be made before a budget can be set.
- Where will you perform?
- Will the production be produced for performance in a single venue or will it tour to places with different degrees of technical support and equipment?
- How much will it cost and how will you raise the money?
- Are there any conditions attached to the funding that the production must meet?
- Have any of the key performers other contracts in place which will limit their availability for the run of the production?
- How many people will be needed and who will they be? This is the most crucial and making a mistake in this decision, and in the choice of people to form the company, can have repercussions through every aspect of the production.

MONEY MATTERS

It might seem to contradict the artistic nature of the project to place such importance on the financial implications of creative work but theatre-making costs money and its practitioners have to eat. The cost of different projects varies by many thousands of pounds but all are governed by the same rules; the same questions must be asked and answered. The most straightforward way for this process to begin is to work through a list. This list will differ according to the size and nature of the project and the length and cost of it will depend on the expected money available. Allowing for the fees of a casting director may seem an essential to some projects, whereas for others a major expense is paying for the bus tickets of unpaid performers.

It could happen like this ...

The funding for a production is in place. The play has been written, the number and types of people in the cast have been discussed and budgeted for and the auditions have taken place. The lead role calls for an actor with particular skills: as well as carrying a demanding role he must play the violin, have puppeteering skills and the sort of looks that will make him convincing both as a teenager and an old man. It proves impossible to find an actor with all these qualities and the audition process gives the writer the idea of splitting the role into two, so that one actor plays the old man and another the young man. Either of them could then play the violin, and as long as they both have the instinct and the physical ability to learn to animate puppets, the play would be improved by this device. The repercussions to the allocation of the budget are daunting because an extra actor will have to be employed not only for rehearsal but also for the opening run and the ensuing tour.

Young companies without experienced production managers on board may find this list useful as it is easy to overlook a money-eating expense which may have a dramatic effect on the final production. Once the main groups are decided they can be subdivided according to the nature of the project so that each person knows how much money is available to fuel their work.

Fees and Salaries

Directors, designers, makers, stage managers and performers all need to be paid. Impoverished companies may work for the chance to make their ideas happen in public and very little money. Often they work for nothing at all except a hope of a share in the notional profits. This must be seen as hope and not an expectation, as by the time the punters are buying their tickets there will be a long list of people who are entitled to a share. Every effort should be made to find enough in the budget to pay the daily working expenses (travel and food), or at least for coffee, tea, fruit and biscuits in the rehearsal room. Good will and good company feeling can help to compensate for lack of cash. Sets, puppets, costumes, props and objects are obvious expenses. Lighting and special-effects sound, recording fees and all equipment and its transport between venues add to the cost. Phone and communication, petrol and parking and the cost of entertaining the chap who you hope is going to write an article on your production for the local paper all have to be paid for by someone.

Venue Costs

Traditional performance spaces have a set rent which may include the cost of resident technicians. Less conventional spaces may be cheap or free but there might be concealed costs. There may be nowhere to hang the lights, or, in the open air, no electricity supply, which may mean hiring a generator and extra riggers. Insurance, sound equipment, toilets, access for trucks and somewhere for the actors to change all have to be arranged. All these problems, and many more, have solutions, but the solutions cost time and money and must be considered in advance

Casting, Workshop and Rehearsal Costs

Casting, whether it is through workshop sessions or through auditions, needs a venue, a space big enough and preferably anonymous

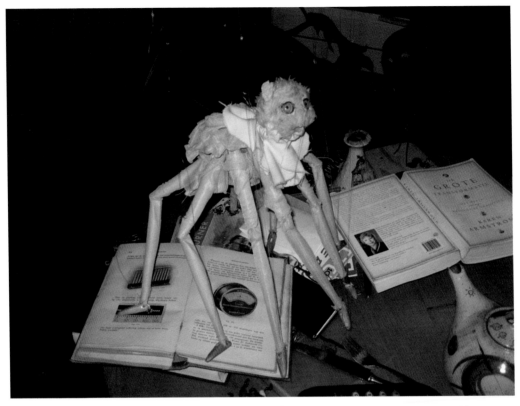

Madam Spider, made by Mirjam Langemeijer, explores an inauspicious venue.

enough for everyone to get the opportunity to create their own atmosphere. Rehearsal space must be booked along with puppets and objects to work with, plus equipment such as a piano. Scripts and travel must be allowed for.

The production manager or stage manager will need a supply of money, actual cash that can be put into the assistant stage manager's hand when they are sent running out to the shops to buy rehearsal props or tea bags. When booking rehearsal space, it is important to make sure that your rights to the use of the space are clearly set out, particularly if it is not a theatre rehearsal room but a church hall or a community centre.

- Do you have exclusive use of the space?
- Is someone going to complain if you make a noise?
- Will equipment be safe if you leave it overnight?
- Are you going to be asked to clear out of the space on Wednesday afternoon for a karate class of nine-year-olds who will play with your props?
- Who is in charge of the space? Get a name and a contact number to deal with the broken key or leaking roof situation.

Advertising
The design and distribution of posters, flyers and programmes, e-flyers, website

Some examples of less obvious clauses in a contract which clarify the responsibilities of the company and the artist:

1.1 Hours for performance days will be dependent upon location of the venue and how long the travel to and from the venue takes; The Artist agrees to accept the start and finish times as outlined by The Company.

1.2 Performances in any given seven-day period will not exceed five. Some performances (To Be Confirmed by the Theatre Company) will include a commitment from The Artist to participate in a Question and Answer session, either pre or post performance and The Artist agrees to comply with these requests from The Company.

1.3 The Company will cover The Artist's travel and accommodation costs for the Out-of-London performances and will pay an additional £15.00 per diem to the Artist for the performance days.

information, production photographs and any information sent to the press can use a considerable proportion of the production expenses. This advertising and production information is most important, even to a small fringe company, if it wants to be taken seriously. The Internet makes it possible to spread information about productions and companies to an ever-widening public and it's worth forking out money and using up time to make a good website. It is to be hoped, of course, that the money spent on this will be repaid by an equal increase in box office takings, the sale of pro-

grammes and the revenue from people advertising in the programme. However, that money comes later and it's no good waiting until the play has opened to advertise it.

Administration
Even if the production office is a table and a computer in someone's bedroom there will still be running costs: phones, stationery, ink cartridges and stamps, plus cups of coffee in nearby cafés for the PR meeting that you don't want to happen in your bedroom. Any sort of entertaining, sometimes necessary as a PR exercise, is expensive. A proper office and staff boost the costs further. Contracts, insurance, fees payable for the use of scripts and the housekeeping expenses of cleaning and fuelling the office have to be paid for by someone.

Contracts
The contract is an important document, not just because it sets out money matters, but also because it makes clear the responsibilities of both parties to the project. A clause in the contract for a touring production that states it is the responsibility of the artist to turn up in time to catch a train or plane may save the company a last-minute expensive train fare; an artist would want to know whether or not the company will be responsible for their overnight expenses or whether they will spend a proportion of their fee on accommodation. It is best to be forewarned before a bad experience teaches you to be wary when writing or signing contracts.

Contingency
Most projects cost more than expected and unfortunately only experience and a track record will give you a clue as to how much money your production is likely to make at the box office. However, experience and a track

record are not always reliable, so it is best to be prepared. It is essential to build into your budget a contingency allowance of a minimum of 10 per cent for all the things you haven't thought of or could not have known about in advance. More if you can manage it. Keep quiet about it where possible or every department will lay claim to it. If it is left over (which it won't be) at the end, you will have no trouble using it profitably.

Fund-Raising

Fund-raising takes time and must be started well before the first rehearsal; it can be useful to create a schedule as a guideline. Look at the ideas for the show with a cold and calculating eye and see if there are any factors that will encourage companies or individuals to invest, sponsor or financially support your show. Grants are there for the Arts, but it is worth studying their criteria carefully so that you do not waste time applying for something outside their remit. The Internet has become an excellent tool for tracking down potential funders – type in 'grants for the arts' or some such phrase and when you have tracked down a list, check through to see what might apply to your idea. You may believe with your whole heart in the value of your project to the Arts and the community, but it is a particular skill to convince others that your faith rests on firm foundations. They will want facts, and they will want a long time to assess those facts, so start as early as you can. Less enlightened funding bodies tend to look at anything involving puppets as being work for an audience of children and are not familiar with object or visual theatre at all, so be extra clear about your target audience when applying.

R&D workshops can help the fund-raiser by providing a tangible idea and some visual images of the likely growth of the project. One of the main difficulties of obtaining funding for this sort of project is finding a solid hook to attract backers. Excitement, enthusiasm and belief in the project carries more weight than you might imagine in backing discussions, but it is much easier to enthuse credibly if you have something tangible to enthuse about.

It may sound cold-hearted to approach creative work from a calculated financial angle, but it happens, and happens a lot. The group can look at current funding and slant the angle of the work to fit into its letterbox. Perhaps the local authority has money available to promote work that involves young people in the ethnic roots of their community; a project may be devised that, while using the talents of the company, is angled to slot into the criteria of the funders. It is always better, when approaching bodies for funding, to find out the name of the person who deals with the type of work you are planning and to build a relationship with them. It's easy to spend weeks in a situation where nothing at all happens because your paperwork has scattered around different desks and no one person feels a connection with your project. Follow up applications with a phone call to make sure they have been channelled to the right port.

THE CREATIVE TEAM

The weight of talent in a creative team involving puppet or object work is not selected or distributed in the same way as it would be in a naturalistic production of a conventional play. The director of the piece has the delicate and demanding job of fusing all the talents in the team and making sure that they all travel along the same path to the same goal.

Papier mâché in the workshop.

Designers and Makers

Sets and costumes must be fit for purpose. Scene changes must work smoothly and actors must be able to move in and manage their costumes. Puppet and object design and making boosts these skills up several notches, as the technical subtleties of their designs are complicated, demanding and very, very varied. Think of a hinge. A hinge on a piece of scenery has a straightforward purpose. You can go to an ironmonger's or a hardware shop and look at hinges and choose the one that will fit your purpose. Think of the hinge joint of a knee. Perhaps this knee joint is the size of bucket or the size of a cotton reel or a sugar lump.

Perhaps the two 'bones' of the joint are made of wood or metal or straws. The best hinge for this joint may not be hanging in a size-labelled packet in the shop: it might be the end of an old leather handbag strap, supple with long use; or it could be a strip cut from the packaging of a newly delivered computer, the joint that hinged the pin to the back of a brooch, or a section of industrial fencing. The object to be hinged could be the jaw of a talking lemon or a singing dustbin. Because the problems are so random and bizarre, the people who solve them must have open and searching eyes to root out the solutions. Often the only way to know if something works is to try it and see,

61

and the relationship between designer and maker, where the two jobs are separate, must be full of trust and communication. The designer is likely to spend more time in rehearsal, as the way his or her designs work are too complex and integral to the actors' performances to be left to be sorted out in the technical rehearsal.

Lighting Designers
These creators of magic play a vital part in puppet and object work because as well as creating atmosphere and place, as they do in any production, they show the audience where their attention should be focused. There are things, strings, rods and animators that should not draw the eye, and objects, which may be much smaller, that must demand attention. The lighting for work with shadows must be precise. Though all this is a straightforward problem where there is enough equipment and a place and technicians to rig it, it becomes a more inventive job when you are working on a tight budget in a difficult space.

Sound Designers
The soundscape for puppet/object productions tends to be complex. The entire script is

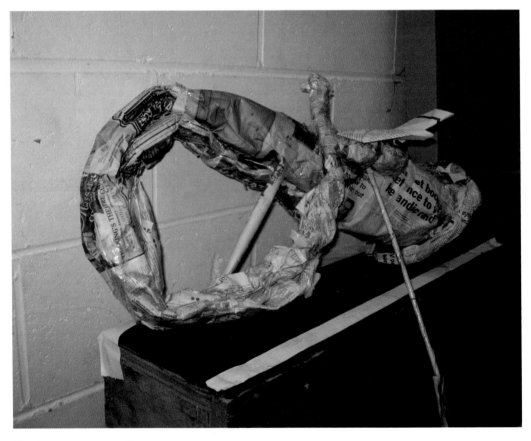

The instrument may be paper ...

... or a shadow... but its sound is brass.

sometimes pre-recorded and the physical performance of the piece is played to the tempo and strengths of this recording. Or the sound may be part-recorded and part-live. Sound designers can have extra demands made of them when working with all larynx-less performers. The use of a soundscape to support the emotional interior life of the characters is often very effective, although this is no more a rule than any other rule in this lawless genre. These composers, also, have an eye for the unusual, for example the plastic drinks bottle that makes a sinister crackle and the human qualities in the sound of instruments. They understand that an oboe is more prone to constipation than a trumpet and a flute more virginal than a cello.

Movement, Music and Animation Directors
The director of a piece, particularly when humans, puppets and objects are performing together, may not specialize in animated work. The presence of other directors on the team with particular skills in other directions can be invaluable. A movement director understands how to help the performers to use their bodies to present the story onstage to the audience. It is not the same as choreographing a dance. Their presence on the team, even if only for a few days of rehearsal, can give the cast a confidence in their ability to move with fluidity and purpose. This trust in their own bodies will be reflected in the way they use the puppets and objects. The same is true of puppeteers and puppet makers. Their experience and skill, whether as part of a company or as an additional director, will speed the process whereby actors learn to give the objects life and movement. A music director, not only when singing is involved but also when sounds are used to

63

create the world of the story, gives the same confidence-building results. All this confidence is not just for the sake of the performers – it also gives the audience a better experience.

CREATING THE COMPANY

The company can be cast with an eye to performers having different skills, experience and specializations. The fact that you mean to use those skills should be made clear from the start and on the contract. Actors put their additional skills on their CVs and there will always be some who have movement, puppeteering or musical experience in addition to performing skills. When there is not enough money to employ specialists, it is still possible to assemble a company in which the performers use their specialist skills and knowledge to lead the rest of the company in workshops.

Casting and Crewing
Casting for object and visual theatre is as crucial as for any production, but it works slightly differently because those casting are not just looking for performers to fill particular roles. Choosing the company is influenced by the core members of the team wanting to work with people whose work they know and trust. Producers have directors and writers they trust. Directors have designers and performers they work with on a regular basis, and those designers have makers whose work they know and like. Movement directors and composers, stage managers and production managers and, of course, actors, animators and puppeteers will all be suggested.

The rest of the company will be selected through interview, or an audition that is likely to take the form of a practical workshop. The selection does not depend solely on the ability of the artist. Most puppet and object work is collaborative, so it is no good employing the most talented and experienced puppeteer for a devised piece if they do not enjoy collaboration, or the most talented actor if they cannot transfer the audience's attention from themselves to the puppet.

The experimental nature of rehearsals for most of this type of work will need technicians, designers and cast to muck in together. Everyone in the company will need the understanding, patience and generosity to stand back or hand over their ideas to anyone with more skill than themselves in any particular area. You are looking for an ability to experiment and learn. You are looking for performers who have a wide base of skills to call on. They must be able to develop and perform their roles but also have good physical skills and improvising ability, and possibly play an instrument and sing. They must also have an ability to breathe life into inanimate objects. Above all, they must be good at trusting the other members of the company and sharing their thoughts and ideas. It is not possible to be a star in this sort of work, or to stand back from the messier side of production.

AT WORK

Once the company, large or small, is assembled, more exciting discussions can begin. Devised puppet and object work, and the more visually inspired branches of theatre, often grow from a director/designer partnership, or a group of director/composer/designer/choreographer who have found a way of working together where each feeds into, and feeds from, the work of the others. There must always be trust, understanding and a mutual respect for each other's work. Much of the early discus-

It could happen like this ...

The skills that the piece demands must be clear in the minds of those responsible for the casting before they make a short list of auditionees. Perhaps a potential cast list would look like this:

- actor, male, playing age 25–35; needs good puppeteering skills
- actor, male, playing age 60+; must be physically supple and have bass-baritone singing range
- actor, female, playing age 18–23; must be light enough to work on actor's shoulders as giant
- actor, male or female, to play numerous parts, animate puppets and scenery.

The company will also be hoping for at least two instrument players and a movement specialist within the cast.

A casting workshop might be run like this:

- A short list of performers will meet in a rehearsal room with the director and members of the team who are close to the core of the production. The make-up of this selection committee (which will be much less formal than it sounds) will vary with the nature of the project. There may be a musical or choreographic director. A performer/puppeteer who has already been cast may be there to work with the candidates. There may be puppeteers in the group who have bought puppets with them and others who have little past experience of animating objects.
- After the introductory warm-up there must be some exercise that will show if the performers have a natural ability to work with objects. Perhaps everyone will be given an empty mug (a useful choice as the handle can stand in for a nose). The way the group breathes life into the object-character they invent will show as the mugs meet and talk to each other and behave in improvisations of different situations. At the end of these exercises there will be a pretty clear picture of the physical, vocal and imaginative ability of the candidates.
- A new short list can be made for individual auditions.

Giving a newspaper creature life in an animation exercise.

sion will be concerned with making sure that the key members of this creative team agree about the content, genre and general shape of the work they are about to start making.

Production Meetings

Production meetings make sure that all the practical aspects of the show will happen on time and within budget. These meetings will happen at regular intervals throughout the rehearsal period and may concern the whole company or a smaller core of key workers. The meetings may consist of twenty or more people all busily concerned with their own aspects of the production: directing, designing, stage managing and creating the set and music, light and sound; puppet, prop, costume and mask makers and as many others as there is work to keep them busy and money to pay them. Or a meeting may consist of two or three people who are performers as well as back-stage workers. Whatever the situation, disaster will strike if someone isn't responsible for making sure that everyone, the great big group or the hard-pressed trio, knows what they are supposed to be doing, when they're supposed to be doing it and how much money they can spend. It is remarkably easy, even in a

Suggestions for improvisation and exploration in the rehearsal room.

Discussion of a knotty problem in the script.

small company, to find that three people have been struggling and using up valuable time to find a solution to the same problem because they simply haven't realized what's happening. Such as situation is wasteful, irritating and disappointing, and all because of a failure of communication.

Controlled, communicative and careful production meetings have a particularly strong role to play in any performance process. Where the work is devised by the company, they are the vital link between the creation of ideas and the people who have the practical responsibility of making them happen. Without these meetings, the exciting and inventive work that has engrossed everyone in the rehearsal room would never see the light of the stage. The most wonderful ideas can vanish because the organization and communication that makes them come true have not been put in place. It can be hard to find time for a production meeting when urgent work waits in the rehearsal room or workshop, but they are necessary. It is all very well for a lighting effect of the most magical power to be imagined during rehearsal, but if nobody tells

67

the lighting designer, the audience will never get to be enchanted by its wonder. And there may be no time left, at the last moment, to order the effect and get it delivered in time, and no money left in the budget to pay for it even if it can be obtained.

Even the most informal production meeting needs an agenda and one person who makes sure all the points on the agenda have been addressed. Everyone has stuff to talk about and everyone wants to talk; the object of the meeting is to make sure the necessary stuff is sorted out and the rest is dropped without time-wasting. People involved in the puppet and object theatre world are passionate and imaginative about their work. The agenda, and its cool-headed keeper, is needed to make sure the points are covered and the meeting doesn't go on all night.

The rehearsal period tends to be long, even in a low-budget production, because each day's rehearsal will throw up new ideas; indeed, it can seem as if there would be no end to the process if the date for the opening night was not set and the company had enough money to keep them going. Pre-production preparation has a different emphasis for every one of the team.

Designer
It is almost impossible to separate the design brief from its practical realization, the design ideas from the inspiration and invention of the performer, and the design realization from the technical know-how that will support its appearance onstage. So the preparatory work must set as much as can be managed in place, while trying to keep as many opportunities open as possible. Research can be done in advance. The designer can look at the subject matter and guess what further information

will be needed, for example about Hannibal crossing the Alps. Supplies of stuff that might be used can be sourced and priced, such as carbon-fibre rods, smoke capsules or arctic camouflage netting. Workspaces can be sorted out and ideas and possibilities discussed with the rest of the team. It may be necessary, if rehearsal time is short, to begin work on stuff that is likely to be used, while trying to leave enough leeway in the design for changes and invention during rehearsal. But it is vital not to get everything decided upon and ready, because it will more than likely change, and change for the better.

The budget should also be viewed with a clear and not too optimistic eye. It is always easy to spend more if it becomes available, but it can be destructive to invent when the realization of those inventions cannot be paid for. There is a sort of see-saw balance between knowing something is absolutely impossible for the company and venue (for example, a huge projected cyclorama of clouds with a complex ballet of shadow gods and heroes) compared with a beautiful but achievable effect (a shadow play on a screen within the set). It is not always a good idea to let the impossible ideas out into the open, as it can make people long for the grand idea and be less excited and supportive of the idea that is actually possible. The big idea can always be saved for that golden moment in the future when there will be a huge space, splendid technology and a massive budget to play with.

When it comes to working in this sort of theatre there is often no clear division between set and object, or object and costume. If different designers are working on all three, they will need constant close collaboration. If outside makers are used to bring the designs to life they will need to work closely with the

It could happen like this ...

The object, a life-sized car, is designed. The idea is that as the doors, windows, boot and bonnet open, the car transforms in various ways into a house, a smoke-erupting monster, a cave under the sea and the doorways and passages through which actors struggle to pass from one scene to another, and so on. The car is, in fact, the set as well as an object, a puppet, an entrance and an exit. The workshop makes the car, an expensive and lengthy process. It is brought to the rehearsal room and assembled in its new situation. The idea emerges, as the actors begin to work with it, that the pieces of the car should remain separate – that the whole car can be dismantled and reassembled into alternative shapes during the action and that the backs of all the separate pieces should be fitted with handles so that they can be carried like shields and fitted with clips so that the car can be remade. Because of this, all the pieces have to be light enough to manipulate but the complete car must be larger than life.

The object, so carefully and thoughtfully reproduced from the original design, is returned to the workshop to be taken apart and remade. It takes a special sort of craftsman not to be irritated by these changes. It is always boring taking apart things that you have made. It is difficult to remake them as neatly and as well as the first time. The marks of the alterations, which might not show on stage, glare brightly in the unforgiving workshop. It can seem as if the work is being undervalued and that the design changes should have been sorted out earlier. This dissatisfied feeling makes most people less helpful and positive in their attitude to their work and to yours.

Such difficulties vanish, or at least become much less important, if the makers as well as the designers spend some time in rehearsal and see why things need to change, or even suggest the changes. If you can engage their interest in the project you will have access to their informed input and technical know-how. The weird and varied nature of some of the objects invented for productions means that the makers are not necessarily theatrical craftspeople. Stage designers have the advantage that for non-theatrical makers, rehearsal rooms are interesting places and a welcome change in the humdrum working day. Most makers are happy to come to rehearsal and may well suggest ways round problems that would only be found by a specialist in their subject. They are quite likely to become so hooked by the exciting nature of theatre work that you will have a new and highly skilled fellow worker on many projects to come.

There will, of course, be budget issues in changes like this. And that is one of the reasons why decisions must not be made too early. Much time and money would have been saved if there had been a rough version of the car made of scrap wood and cardboard. Even more money and time would have been saved if there had been the equipment in the rehearsal room to bodge up a very rough version of the car in cardboard for the actors to play with. When the real purpose and performance potential of the car had been decided, the final design and working drawing could have been made and given to the workroom.

designers. It is difficult, as a maker, to realize how necessary it is for their work to remain changeable. Makers and technicians working away from the rehearsal room will not necessarily share the same blinkered enthusiasm as those who are experiencing the creation of the project first hand.

6. REHEARSALS

ctors and puppets do not behave in the same way. The rehearsals are not the same either, even for a play that is scripted, cast and designed before the company meet. They share many of the same working practices, and many of the same

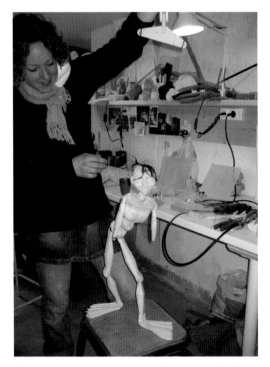

Trying out the movement of a puppet before it is dressed.

problems and excitements, but there is a different emphasis. Puppets may have no inconvenient stomachs and egos but they can't make their own decisions, and there are a lot of issues that must be settled and solved during the rehearsal period.

It does happen, in puppetless theatres, that the designer turns up for the first read-through and is not seen again until the technical rehearsal just before the play opens. He or she will see the actors at costume fittings and the crew to discuss the set and lighting, but will not see a single rehearsal, or any deviation from the way the play was envisaged at the pre-production discussions with the director. It could happen that the puppets remain unchanged and the animators and actors adapt their work to suit the strictures of the puppets, but it is unlikely that a puppet designer/maker will not be a present influence during rehearsals in order to make adjustments as the work develops.

Today's puppets are often part of a cast of actors; actors, as well as puppeteers, will be animating and interacting with the puppets onstage. A director with no particular experience in working with puppets or objects will find advice and help from an experience animator to be invaluable.

THE PROCESS OF REHEARSALS

Rehearsal Preparations

A scripted play makes it possible for the performers to know a lot about the work before they start, for directors to plan and choreograph, and designers and makers to create. Everyone will come to rehearsal with clear expectations.

It may be that the puppets are finished, dressed and strung, a stage is in place, the script written and soundtrack planned if not recorded. In this case, it is likely that the performers will be experienced puppeteers, the director used to working with puppets and the puppets working as the major performers in the piece. Directors and designers may have been working together for some time; the puppets and objects may have been designed and made, waiting laid out in the rehearsal room to meet the actors.

Puppets wait to meet their puppeteers:
RIGHT: *Venus and Adonis wait in their boxes.*
BELOW: *an armed rabbit waits in the wings.*

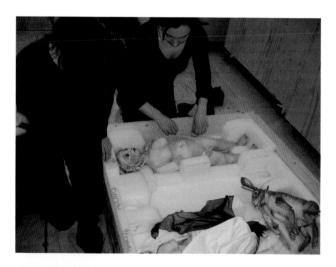

A play which uses puppets and humans working together will be likely to be cast with actors who have varied degrees of experience of working with puppets. They will need puppets for use in rehearsal, preferably ones that are quite like those they will use in performance. In all situations, the performers of a puppet/object performance must have some puppets or objects to hand. The finished condition of these varies depending on the method of performance creation.

You would not expect to find in the rehearsal room of an object theatre play many of the inventions that will appear on the stage in the performance. There will be equipment such as cloth, string, gaffer tape and sticks, as well as a jumble of props and household objects, and puppets left over from other performances. The purpose of all this stuff is to give the performers something more tangible than their own imaginations to play with; it can also give designers, makers and directors a way of showing what is in their minds. It is as instinctive for the creators of this genre of theatre to use objects for inspiration as it is for dancers to use music; if these toys are not provided they will use coats or water bottles, books, chairs,

Objects to stimulate improvisation should have some loose relation to the subject matter: a collection for the modern household.

oranges or anything that is lying around to play with.

The First Rehearsal

The company rehearsing a scripted play may arrive at the first rehearsal to find the puppets designed, made and waiting for them. This first meeting of animator and puppet is taken seriously by all concerned. The animators and actors will be introduced to their puppets and have time to become familiar with their manoeuvrability and their weight. But that is only half the story. The puppets have their own characters, and it takes time and commitment to understand the life that lies hidden in its body and to establish a relationship between puppet and puppeteer. If you have never tried it, put on a mask and stare at yourself in a mirror; the mask has no life or character but it has the power to change the way that you feel about yourself as you stare at your reflection. Something as simple as putting a sock on your hand, concentrating on it in the mirror and moving its 'mouth' will show you that it stops being your own hand and pushes its character towards you.

Puppets are full of contradictions. It is not possible to work with a puppet and, when the

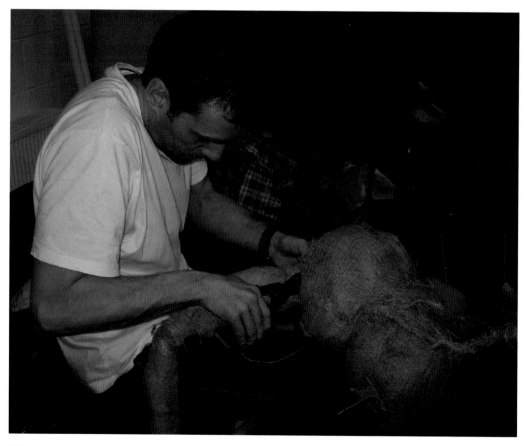

Taking the pliers to a puppet during a pause in rehearsal.

moment of performance is finished, shove it in the corner as if it were an old saucepan. In theory, there is nothing wrong with treating it as a thing without feelings. It can't feel pain or humiliation. But this inanimate object has absorbed something of the spirit of its makers and animators and it feels wrong to endanger it or treat it without respect. This rather spiritual approach vanishes when the puppet needs mending and a nail is whacked into its thigh. The animation is equally contradictory, particularly in rehearsal. The puppeteer is presenting the puppet to the audience. His or her concentration is on the puppet and all the audience's attention is being directed to the puppet. But the puppeteer must also be conscious all the time of how members of the audience are seeing the puppet, whether their interest and emotions are aroused and whether they can understand the message of the puppet's gestures and how on earth the jumble of humans, puppets and props backstage is to be negotiated.

Backstage Choreography

The backstage choreography of a puppet play is complicated for director, animator and stage management. Even when there is enough room in the wings or on the bridge, which never seems to happen, people and puppets engage in a silent backstage performance which is as carefully rehearsed and set as anything the audience sees on stage. Puppets may have several people animating them at one time. One person may be lifting the hand of one puppet and the foot of another. It is quite usual, backstage, to see three or four people huddled in a tight group, arms legs and bodies overlapping as they perform the moves that will appear to belong to one creature onstage.

It could happen like this ...

There is a column glowing in the light which appears to the audience to be a solid cylinder of stone reaching from stage floor to flies. There is a sound: it might be water in the distance; a light pattering; an invisible crowd breathing *hshhhshhh*. A figure walks behind the column and we see him through solid stone. A strange heap begins to develop at the foot of the column. An actor fills a bowl at the column and carries it away. Another actor holds his hand in the column to collect water to splash his face. We see in the lighting change, no longer stone, but water breaking its pouring path over his hand. Other light and the action remind us of the sands of time passing through a giant hourglass. The sounds and the sights are translated to fit the suggested themes. Is it still or is it moving? The audience changes its mind with the suggestions of the action.

None of it is true. The column, the water and the sand are an illusion of most basic technology and precise lighting, sound and acting. Invisible above the stage a slanting plastic tube, with a long slit the width of the column near its lower end, is hung horizontally. A sheet of salt crystals pours steadily though the slit to the stage floor. The magic is all in the way the audience's thoughts and eyes are directed, and the actors, who cannot see the magic, must trust in the director to inform them when their actions tell the right story and when an unconsidered gesture breaks the illusion. Directors of this sort of effect are designers as well.

There will be hooks and stands, shelves and tables where each puppet must be placed to be free and easily graspable for its next appearance. The audience never sees this performance but it can take as long to rehearse as an onstage scene.

Director and Designer/Maker

The role of the designer changes when the inventive process of discussion and rehearsal replaces the script in the post as the stimulus for ideas. Lighting, sound, puppet, object, set and costume designers all work together to enhance the pictures the audience sees. The whole production will grow together towards the first performance. The director conducts and controls the process and the designers build the picture.

A director without the support of all these designers will have to keep track of all the different aspects of performance. Some practitioners find this the perfect way to work. It is possible, in the world of puppetry, to create and perform the whole piece. One man can be emperor and slave, alcoholic and child, bird and horse. He can write the script, design and make the puppets and animate them in his own set, keeping a total control over the project that is not possible on a stage inhabited by actors. Of course, he'll need to be skilled at many different arts and have a personality that feels more confident in his own solo skills than in collaborative work with other practitioners. This solo work creates intense and distinctive performances suffused with the undiluted passion of their creator.

DEVISED WORK

The creation of puppets and objects for a performance which is being devised will grow out of the rehearsal process. There will be no script to work from, or if there is it will only be used as a stimulus for the invention that will follow.

It could happen like this ...

The designer has a work table equipped with the sort of materials that will encourage the making of puppets and objects that fit in with the textures, colours and general feeling envisaged for onstage. The designer and the team have made examples, before the start of rehearsals, of the types of props and puppets likely to become part of the performance. More ideas become apparent through the process of rehearsal and everybody in the company will begin to create the things they want and need to use. Some people will be more eager and able than others at converting their ideas into a practical form, but the attempt, even if it turns out that they are simply making a rehearsal prop, will clarify its structure and use to everyone.

The advantage of this hands-on method of working is particularly clear when experienced puppeteers are working with actors who are not used to performing through a puppet or object; an understanding grows of how to speak through it to the audience; working alongside someone who really understands the genre teaches everyone more than any more formal instruction could ever do. It also gives actors an affectionate relationship with the things they have made and a determination to make them perform. It also opens a door to the new and surprising ideas that come so often from someone who is unfamiliar with the accepted way of working with objects.

There will be an outline story or theme that can be discussed at pre-production meetings, but there may be no certainty which characters will be human and which will be puppets, or how the objects will be used. If the rehearsals are leading to a definite scheduled series of performances, a decision will have been made as to whether the performance will be a puppet show or whether there will be a mixture of puppets, objects and humans telling the story. The show will have been cast and a decision will have been made as to whether puppeteers will be employed to animate the puppets and objects, or whether actors will work both as the characters and the animators.

The Pre-Production Workshop

One way of preparing the ground for the future is to run a development workshop for experimental work around the subject. Puppet and object designer/makers for devised productions can, during the early meetings, gather information about the shape of the work, the proposed audience and the envisaged genre. This information will help them to collect a jumble of objects and equipment for use in rehearsal as improvised mock-ups of the puppets and objects for the final performance. These stand-ins should not be finished or too suggestive of character or form; they are toys to pretend with and a powerful aid to communication between the rehearsing animator and the designer and director.

Sticks and sticky tape, string and different weights of cloth and paper can all be bundled or glued into shape to suggest in the broadest way possible the future form of the puppet or object that will be manipulated in performance. Tubes of stretchy cloth, such as Lycra or Elastane, of different widths can be threaded on hands, feet and bodies, or can cover lumps of newspaper to create shape and size. The result may have little visual connection with the finished object that the audience will see, but will give clear signs of the ways in which they will be animated and the natural strengths of the animators. This information can be discussed after rehearsals and will be distilled into the final design.

The process becomes most productive when the actor/animator and the designer develop a creative working relationship. The animator knows the life and messages the object should convey to the audience and the way it must move to facilitate the effects; the designer imagines and creates the picture the audience will see. When the two points of view are combined, the strongest possible message is given to the audience by a puppet or object.

Playing with Objects

It is difficult to talk about any sort of devising process without relating it to play. It can sound

A performer uses hat, cardboard and scissors to help create a character and a puppet.

a bit coy, but becomes less so when you think of the intense concentration and focused power and energy that children put into playing. And how much they invent and learn while they are enjoying themselves. Improvisation, experiment, inventions of actions and music and the visual pleasures of performance are adult versions of that instinct to find a way to give internal human thoughts and feelings an open and concrete reality that can be shared with others.

The beginning of serious rehearsals for devised work starts with play. Play with bodies and objects, words and music. Once bodies and voices are loosened and ready, anything lying around the rehearsal room becomes fuel for the work. So it is quite a good ploy for the person who is going to be designing and making the props and puppets to make sure the things lying around the place bear some relevance to the subject matter of the work. It will soon become clear that some of the stuff is used in the daily work, while some is tried and rejected. The refining process that will create the actual prop will be based on the rehearsal process and the way the prop's meaning will be read by the audience. A lump of scrunched paper dumped in someone's baseball cap for rehearsal will be refined into a crinkled ball of red wool in a saucepan for the actual jam-making scene.

There is usually an underlying joke in this sort of improvisation that keeps the working atmosphere buoyant and good-humoured. It helps to dispel any over-analytical tendencies which are best kept to sessions at the beginning and end of the working day as they tend to weigh down the flights of invention. The

A vocal warm-up before rehearsal starts.

Woollen jam boiling in a saucepan.

work is concentrated and intense, like all good play; it needs to burst out into laughter or the whole thing starts to internalize, with the accompanying danger of forgetting that it is all for an audience and not an intellectual or a therapeutic exercise.

Working with Performers in Rehearsal

There is no doubt that designing and making the puppet or object during rehearsal adds another layer of fluidity to the way the animator controls the object. Everyone, even actors whose training teaches them to adopt the movement of the characters they play, has their own particular way of manipulating their voice and body. When an actor creates a character, they use the basis of their own natural movement as a sponge to absorb the movement of the role being created. The animator does the same thing, but with an added layer of separation, in that they are working through a body created by a puppet maker's interpretation of his role. This sounds as if it could make the job of assuming a role more difficult, but the apparent complication hides a huge advantage: the animator is free of their own body and

It could happen like this ...

In the story of the play, the archaeologist (played by the puppeteer/actor) is accompanied in her work by a vulture who knows, through the folklore passed down to it from its forebears, the true story she is trying to unearth. In rehearsal, as the story develops, it becomes clear that the vulture is a stroppy, argumentative teenager of a bird and the archaeologist is a serious professor. At the start of rehearsals, the bird is represented by a sock on the actor's hand. It becomes clear, throughout the day's work, that it will be awkward if the glove puppet is taken off and put on during the course of the onstage action; the feeling being searched for is that of the bird flying down from the sky when it wants to butt in on the action.

The following day's rehearsal begins with the designer giving the performer an old sweater with the now toeless sock tacked onto one sleeve. She can wear the sock on her wrist, or with a single movement pull the sleeve over her knuckles and make a beak of fingers and thumb and the puppet will appear and sit on her arm in the blink of an eye. All fine and dandy but it is still an old sweater, a holey sock and a couple of safety pins and not ART. Nonetheless, from the point of view of the animator, it works and she is able to feel the character of the vulture in her arm and the character of the archaeologist in the rest of her body.

The actual puppet that will be used in performance can be made using the information gathered from the sweater and old sock approach. A costume will be designed that will allow the odd-shaped sleeve that will occasionally become the vulture while looking acceptable as an everyday garment. The costume will also need to be made in plenty of time for the inevitable adjustments that will become necessary during later rehearsals.

For further information about the Museum performance in Aguilar del Rio Alhama, visit www.tallerspiral.com

can creep or leap according to temperament into a new shell; a shell full of possibilities.

Every animator has a particular strength; a way of working or a type of puppet that lends itself to their most natural style of working. An experienced animator or puppeteer will, of course, be practised at working with all sorts of puppets. They will have mastered the ability to transfer character away from themselves and into the object under all sorts of conditions. But there will be some features, some methods and some objects that make this transference particularly easy and natural.

The designer must discover this particular bond and try to incorporate it into the objects he or she is designing. The cooperative interaction which takes place in an R&D workshop gives space and time for this to happen and it's a terrible waste not to grab the opportunity for interactive work. Everyone creates their best work when they have the right tools and the right atmosphere to work in. The communication that encourages exchange of information makes it possible to create the best environment and tools. Listening and looking is as important, if not more important, than talking. Watching an actor or animator, how they move, how they shift focus away from their own body and mind and into the bundle of rags and sticks that is the rehearsal stand-in enables the

Animators and makers working together on the technicalities of a giant wing.

designer to bodge up a more project-appropriate bundle of rags and sticks. Watching for five silent minutes may reveal more than a three-hour conversation. The toughest barrier to communication in the devising workshop is the defensive behaviour we adopt to protect our ideas and when learning to trust the ideas of others. Avoiding the formation of this barrier is as much a design skill as drawing. The final design and form of the puppet should reflect a cooperative creative approach.

PLANNING AND DECISION

The days of rehearsal create the material of the piece and shape it into a performance. Companies work to a schedule that makes sure all the sections and disciplines have been covered. A devised piece may be planned in advance, but will be subject to change as the progress of the work grows clear. There comes a point in this whirlwind of ideas and invention when the director or directors have to reclaim control of the work and shape it for the performance. There may be music, movement and design-based directors as well as the general director more usual in theatre performance, and they have been working in part throughout the rehearsals as instigators and encouragers of invention.

Giant birds up the mountain. When the birds lie flat on the ground they vanish in the lie of the land; when they are raised up they can be seen for miles.
Photos: Chris Baldwin

The line which will run through the show – the path of the narrative, the pattern and shape, the stresses and calms – must be reclaimed and refashioned into a work that will draw the audience through from the first moment to the last and make certain they will stay engaged all along the path.

Shaping the Ideas into a Performance

A good percentage of the early rehearsal time will have been spent in encouraging an anarchic freedom in the rehearsal room. A usual pattern of work would begin with a strenuous vocal and physical warm-up, then erupt into work around topics related to the subject matter. Discussion and experiment, jokes and exaggerations will all have been encouraged as the trust and freedom between the performers, and the inclusion of puppets and objects in their work, develops.

But at some point the director or directors must take control, or the audience will become sidelined by the delight the performers take in their invention. This is a tricky point in the rehearsal process. In every devised performance there comes a moment when the territorial rights of the director are demanded and conceded. This sounds pretty harsh and undemocratic, but, even where the moment is so subtle as to be almost unnoticed, it occurs. And the success of this moment, as long as the director is good at the job, determines the successful curve of the play from start to finish.

Control becomes even more important when there is no script to shape the structure of the piece. An unspoken agreement has to be established that the final decision lies with the directors. Ideas that interrupt the structure and flow of the work will have to be chucked away, however good they may be in their separate selves. Lengthy discussions and experiments that interrupt the flow of the work have to be curtailed. Decisions, many of which will involve set, costume lighting and sound cues, have to be made and stuck to.

There is a school of thought which feels that performance-making is a democratic procedure and all the voices in its creation should have equal rights. But, like any other democracy, someone is needed to collect the opinions, manage the money, see to the technical necessities and take the flak if it all goes wrong. Otherwise the audience will be paying to see something that scarcely concerns them at all, and is, in effect, an actors' experiment.

7. THE WORK OF THE DESIGNER/MAKER

Some designers make everything they design. They like and need the total control that this gives them over their work; they are also often the writers and performers of the work. They develop a style of performance that allows them to bring their ideas to life and those they work with support their inspiration. This intense and often solitary work can have a long gestation. Such work demands total immersion in the subject. So much time and emotional effort is invested in its creation that the work, when completed, may remain in the repertoire of its creator for some time.

Others pass their ideas to specialists to create. They visualize the way the puppets will look, their faces, clothes and means of expression, and have a practised ability to communicate visually and verbally the pictures in their heads. They might model the head in clay and pass it to a woodcarver to copy; they might design the body and its workings and leave the costume to another designer. They may make precise working drawings, or explain the movement and weight they want in the puppet, or demonstrate with their own bodies the movement they want to recreate. The work will be reviewed as it goes along to make sure that,

when it is finished, is will be a fusion of their original idea and the technique and understanding of the maker. They may make experimental and unfinished try-outs until a mutual understanding has been reached. Effort and time go into perfecting a good designer/maker relationship and once both are sure of its success, the relationship may continue through many different projects.

The ones who lie between these two extremes do a mixture of both, and their experience in the job has led them to a style of making that suits their creative drive. The work of an experienced designer/maker carries their personal signature in the fusion of instinct and craft. Work that involves objects tends to be closely allied to the performers' physical skills and invention, often being developed from the work in rehearsal.

WHAT MAKES A MAKER/ANIMATOR?

Puppet Makers
The makers of puppets and objects are animators and puppeteers, artists, carvers and welders, sculptors, mould-makers and scavengers, in fact anyone who wants and needs

Working on a vulture with old fishing baskets, papier mâché and silk.

to, and can, translate the essence of a character or a feeling into the work. Some of the work is crafted with such skill and delicacy that the puppets seem to be asleep when lying in the wings before a performance. Others may be little more than an old suitcase with a false bottom that could be chucked in the bin by an unwary cleaner.

Sculpture, graphic arts, engineering, costume or prop making, acting and dance, even the world of fashion, have all produced these designers and makers. The genre is so varied in size and content and so dependent on the creative input of the designer/maker that there is room for endless different perspectives in the creation and practice of ideas. There may seem at first sight to be no connection between the gigantic, combustible castle that will explode in the pyrotechnic fury of a fire-breathing dragon high on a Devon hill and the tiny toy

*Puppet designer and maker
Lyndie Wright at the Little
Angel Theatre.*
LEFT: *The team in the work-
room.*
BELOW: *A pinboard of ideas.*

The workbench.

At work on a bear's fur.

theatre, perfect in every Victorian detail, where the stage is no bigger than an open book. But the creators of these productions, however far apart are the starting points for their work, all believe in the power of puppets to stir the imaginations and emotions, and have confidence that in the right hands these images made of paper, cloth, leather, wood and resin, can engage the audience in a unique and powerful experience.

Many makers are skilled animators and this skill is employed in the development of the construction of their puppets. A maker will animate the puppet all through the creative process to see how it moves and takes on the character it will assume in performance. It makes puppeteers happy if they can talk to the maker about ideas for movements that arrive during rehearsal and instigate the little adjustments that will make those moves possible. The business of learning the trade is as varied as the people who do the job.

The Accomplished Art of Seeing Possibilities
Anything, in the world of visual theatre, can acquire a character. One of the great arts of the job of designing such productions is the ability to see everyday objects with an innocent eye, an eye that can look into the cupboard under the stairs and see a vacuum-cleaner monster, a despairing lover of a jacket on a coat hook and the comic and varied creatures, or perhaps the collection of emotions, that can hop or creep out of the basket of hats

---

It could happen like this ...

Aristophanes' *The Birds* is rehearsing for a performance in an abandoned school and its garden in a remote Spanish village. The first meeting makes it clear that the performance must be accessible to all ages and enjoyable by a public unused to theatre. It has to have an air of fiesta and carnival about it to encourage everyone to come, including those who would not book tickets for a conventional theatre performance. The company includes puppeteers, musicians and actors, but all the performers must make and animate puppets, play instruments and act.

The director wants to use objects and materials that are familiar to the audience to create the piece of theatre. Time and money are limited and the designer spends most of the budget on lengths of silk in bright, clear colours and relies on the local environment to provide the rest. She makes a collection of materials from the surrounding fields and creates a rough mock-up of a puppet bird. The more experienced puppeteers in the company play with the bird; they pinpoint its advantages and its limitations and suggest modifications.

A day is set aside for a workshop where the company will make their own puppets. The coloured silk and the collection of bamboo, withies, old hosepipe and twine are laid out, and the cast make and work out how to animate their own puppets with the advice and help of the experienced puppeteers in the company. As the actors work through the rehearsal period towards the first performance, they pick up and use other materials organic to the countryside, adapting the pattern to suit their preferred way of animation. By the time the actors perform, their puppets are their own and unique, despite the similarity in pattern and material.

For further information about Spirál's production of Aristophanes' The Birds, *visit www.tallerspiral.com*

It could happen like this ...

In a college in France student puppeteers are at work in a studio. Their teachers are sculptors, puppeteers, directors, scriptwriters and practitioners from the professional world. Each student has a stool, a workbench with a shelf above and a pinboard. Every one of these nineteen spaces shows a different approach to the same work. Some of them will end up as animators and some as makers of puppets for others. Their background training is as varied as their creative drive. Painters, dancers, mime artists, street performers and actors all work together to study both the traditions and innovations of puppetry. They have access to a resource centre and library where the work of other practitioners is available for study. The tools in the workshop next to the design studio help them to build the puppets and objects they invent; a costume studio above provides the equipment and technical help to dress their puppets.

In this one studio, where everyone is given the same training, that there is no 'house style'. Along one row of workbenches, one student makes tiny, simple figures from corks and wire, another works on the stringing of a tall, frog-footed marionette, a third works on a lifelike clay face which will become the face of a puppet of himself, another makes a strange creature whose stomach opens up to reveal its past life and in the far corner the coat collar of a glove puppet is being adjusted with needle and thread. The atmosphere is concentrated and hard-working, but not silent. People share ideas and suggest alterations. Everybody gathers round to see how an important stage in the development of one student's idea has succeeded. There is chat and laughter as well as serious discussion.

These students at the Institut International de la Marionette in Charleville-Mézières have the opportunity to study their craft in the most encouraging surroundings, where invention and new ideas are as important as the technique which supports them; they all appreciate how fortunate they are to be there.

For further information about the Institut International de la Marionette, visit www.marionnette.com

The students of the puppet school at Charleville-Mezières. LEFT: At their workbench.

It could happen like this ...

The students of the puppet school at Charleville-Mezières.
LEFT: *In the puppet wardrobe.*
BELOW RIGHT: *At work on a new idea.*
BELOW LEFT: *casting a head.*

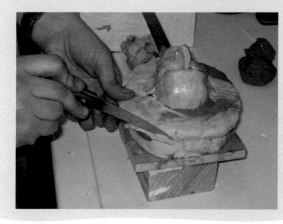

An agavi leaf beak.

Testing controls made of withies, old hosepipe and string.

A performer making a puppet.

First flight.

All the birds at rest before the show. Photo: Chris Baldwin

and gloves. A walk on the street can reveal a hidden message in a half-unstuck poster hanging one-eyed from a billboard, or sinister intent in the single black umbrella in the bobbing sea of colours at the station exit, an umbrella that could, perhaps, kill or flirt, peck or cause a caressing draft on a cheek. It may sound strange, but it's only a different way of linking your eyes to your brain and storing information for future use; not so far from linking a red traffic light with STOP or mistaking a squeaking hinge for a miaow. In many cases, these found objects will need adaptation, redesigning and remaking in order that they can be animated in performance, but this will come later. The recognition of the possibilities hidden behind the everyday face of these objects is as much of a creative act as is their transformation into stageworthy items.

Rubbish
There are hundreds of possibilities hidden in rubbish. The stuff we consider useless and throw away has a way of giving ideas to inventors of theatre. It may be because it is free; at least you don't have to spend any money to experiment and the fact that the raw materials of your invention are so cheap loosens up the creative process and allows you to try out ideas in the morning that may well be in the bin by

nightfall. Our world today throws so much away that there is a particular satisfaction in rescuing some of this unvalued stuff and making it full of meaning or beauty or comedy.

WHAT TYPE OF PUPPET?

A decision has to be made early on in the creation of a performance as to how the puppet or object will be manipulated. There are practical necessities to be considered. Will the character move its mouth to speak? Must it be able to pick up a prop and hold it? Can one person animate it alone, or will there be occasions when two or three people must work together to create a complicated series of movements?

The puppet has to fit in with its onstage world. The operators may work their magic unseen by the audience, as in a marionette theatre where strings vanish into the hidden area above the stage, or there may be a more open stage where the audience can see, but choose to ignore, the humans animating the characters in front of their eyes. All puppets may appear to move by themselves, or can be animated by a visible operator. There is no limit to the different ways stories can be told with objects, but the choice must be made before the designer and maker can get going on creating the final design. It is necessary to know the amount of movement, and the precision of the movements that must become

Parts of the puppet laid out on the workbench ready to assemble.

possible, in order that the working joints and the positions of attachment to the animator can be decided.

There is as combination of instinct, imagination, understanding and inventiveness in puppet makers that makes them such an extraordinary and varied batch of people. Most of them have a particular viewpoint from which they work most creatively. This does not necessarily mean they create just one type of puppet, but that they, like most other artists, work best when they follow their natural inclination. However, the variety of skills inherent in the work, and the different viewpoints and passions of the people and projects they work on, will give them a wider point of view than that of many other creative practitioners. Without exception, and even when they hide the fact, these makers are passionate about their work. And they are, after all, able to create characters that are not bound by the usual laws of our world.

The size of the puppet must relate to the size of the venue; a hand-sized object will lose all of its detail to an audience member at the back of a large theatre. It is surprising, though, how clearly quite small objects may be seen from a distance when the lighting is good and the colour contrast and silhouette are clear and bold.

The Design

The operators of puppets and objects have to transfer their performance from their own body to that of the puppet. The designer/maker makes this transference possible, and creates not only the object the audience sees and responds to, but also the practical means to make the figure come to life. The first visual images of the designer's invention will be stirred by the character presented by the script or the story.

Character's a loose word in this case; it may not be a person or an animal. In the world of puppet and object theatre, everything, even the most prosaic waste-paper basket, can have a personality. But these clear and exciting first pictures must be subject to the practical fact that however beautiful, fantastical, powerful or apt the creation, a human being has to make it come to life for the audience.

One path is for the designer to create a working drawing that shows the inner 'bones' of the object, the way all the moving parts will function and the way it will be manipulated. There must also be a drawing that will show the object the audience sees. The detail will vary depending on its purpose. If the designer is also the maker, the purpose of the designs will be to show the director and other members of the company what to expect. If the puppet or object will be made by another, or even several other makers, every detail must be clear and precise for the designer to get the effect he or she imagines. Another path is to fiddle and experiment in the workshop and rehearsal till the thing works and then remake it to look right. In practice, the two paths cross and recross each other.

The Maker

It may happen that the designer of the puppet is not skilled in the techniques of the medium envisaged for the finished object; he or she may imagine a marionette of wood, with a carved head, but may not actually be a wood carver. In this case, the designer may do a series of drawings of the head and body; drawings which show both the artistic appearance of the head and body, and technical drawings with exact measurements and construction and positioning of the joints of the body and the way in which it will be animated. Or the

It could happen like this ...

A costume maker is working on a pantomime. The idea develops during rehearsal that the villainous King Rat must have a pet rat to which he confides his evil plans. A toy glove puppet is bought by the stage management and used in rehearsal. Due to the rush and business of the rehearsal period, an assumption is made by the actor playing King Rat and his director that the toy is a stand-in prop, a temporary solution while the real item to be used in performance is being made. The stage management department does not realize the toy rat is unacceptable and it is not until the tech rehearsal, when it's far too late and there is not the spare budget to employ a professional puppet maker, that the mistake is discovered. There's a terrible furore and a certain amount of ill feeling and panic. The stage management has no time to start complicated prop making in the middle of the tech. The actor refuses to work with the toy (which is in truth a hopeless and vague rat) and the only solution is for the wardrobe department to have a bash. With a combination of old leather gloves, bristles chopped out of the stage broom, eyes cut from an old washing-up liquid bottle and a jumbling of all sorts of bits and pieces lying around the wardrobe, the costume maker makes the rat and, while experimenting in front of the mirror with her work, discovers a new and exciting pathway.

designer may sculpt the head, hands and feet in clay or some similar medium which will then be copied by a craftsman.

Such craftsmen and women are rare. They are creating a faithful and lively copy of a design. They are adding their own creative feeling to an idea whose spirit began in the mind of its original creator. To say that they copy is to denigrate the great skill and understanding involved in this sort of work; it is a generous act, and one full of self-control and technical ability, to bring someone else's idea to life.

The Nose

The human nose sits there in the middle of a face. It is obvious and is nearer the watcher than any other feature. But even the biggest, most wrinklable or comic nose fades into unimportance, overwhelmed by the mobile expressions of eyes and mouth .A puppet nose is quite a different matter. It sets the path of a creature's gaze. In many cases, it almost replaces eyes when the puppet needs to appear to direct its attention to another object onstage. It is frequently exaggerated when the features of a puppet are sculpted, to make this focus more apparent. The audience will believe and follow the nose-led glance with more accuracy than it will that of an eye, even when the eye's movements are controlled by the most complex mechanical skill. The animator will use the nose as directly as a pointing finger to show the audience where its attention should land.

The Performer as Maker

It is sometimes possible, if the complications of the puppets and objects allow it, for the performers to have a hand in making the things they use. Most people have fun and feel good when they have made something with their hands, particularly when the working atmosphere doesn't surround the process with an aura of mysterious technical secrets. Actors, particularly those who work in collaborative

A performer altering her puppet to suit her style of animation. Photo: Carol Ruiz Marcos

or devised work, tend to be good at turning their minds and bodies to anything new that crops up in the rehearsal room. They may have never made or used a puppet before, but any stuff that helps them tell stories or create characters is grist to their mill. Most grab the chance to turn their thoughts away from the mental and emotional concentration of building a character to making something tangible which answers a practical purpose. There are advantages to the whole company in their experiments, even if the final versions have to be remade with a more expert skill for the actual performance.

Every designer, maker and actor knows the endless fiddling and problems that crop up when performers begin to work with cos-

tumes, masks, puppets or objects that are awkward to use. The familiar stand-in props used in rehearsal will not have called for the same precision of movement and compromise of ease as the real thing. The solid, physical objects do not have the easy adaptability of the virtual ones, which need only a tweak of the imagination to behave as the animator wants. It takes time and patience, tiny adjustments on the part of the makers, to make the problems vanish.

Often neither actor nor designer have the time and both end up not getting quite the effect they want. But if the actor knows how these things are made, and knows the effect they have on the audience, the depressing compromises melt away. To adapt a puppet body to suit the exact size and movement of a hand, arm and shoulder may take twenty tiny adjustments. When that means arranging twenty separate fittings in a different room with all the attendant appointments with the maker and time out of rehearsal and irritation on behalf of all parties, it may be just not worth the time and effort. But if the performer can sit with his or her puppet when they are not needed on stage, and little by little customize it, a complicated and lengthy procedure slides unnoticed into the busy schedule of the working days. It's one thing to take a pair of scissors to someone else's skilled and careful work; it's quite another to fiddle about, during the longeurs that actors have to put up with during the creation of a show, with your own work and try to make it better.

It takes a particular sort of designer or maker to feel easy about what could be seen as an invasion of their artistic territory. There are lots of designers and makers who couldn't bear to have other people interpreting their ideas, as well as lots of performers who prefer to leave it to the experts and be given a professionally constructed prop and told how to use it. But these actors also tend to prefer to work in the more controlled environment where script and designs have been decided before the start of rehearsal.

8. THE WORK OF THE ANIMATOR

THE AUDIENCE'S VIEWPOINT

When actors talk to each other on stage they can see each other and hear where the words are coming from. The audience can see the actors' mouths moving and know who is talking at any one time. Not all puppets have mouths that move. The puppeteer, animating a puppet that is having a conversation onstage, may not be able to see the object of its focus. They may be working behind a screen or playboard, or manipulating the strings or rods offstage. In some cases, the sound, if live, may give them a clue, but in most cases the direction of these tiny moves, which are so natural to an actor, have to be set and learnt. The director and anyone else watching from the point of view of the audience can see if the conversation looks convincing. It will help the animator if they can watch for a time from the auditorium whilst someone else does their job and animates the puppet. The actors never have the chance to look at their own work as the audience does.

The same is true when rehearsing with objects. The angle of the audience's vision is often crucial. Objects which transform, trick or surprise have to be presented with precision and certainty. It is a bit like placing an imaginary frame round an event to channel the onlooker's eye along the right path. It takes a reliable visual imagination, when you already know how a trick works, to imagine you are seeing it for the first time and do not know the technical reality.

The Attentive Puppet

Puppets must listen, or appear to listen and pay attention to the action onstage. The smallest of movements, some little more than the transference of a thought from the puppeteer to the puppet, will register with the audience; there is an inexplicable but evident difference between a puppet still and attentive on stage, and a puppet still and unfocused. It may sound far-fetched. We all know there is no real life in sticks, wood, cloth and metal. But the inattention of a puppet is as blatant as the inattention of an actor, and as detrimental to the action. A state of constant readiness, even when absolutely still, takes continuous concentration from the animator. Puppets are even better than humans at drawing attention to themselves onstage and the animator has to be economical and aware that a slight movement during a period of stillness can tell a story, but can also draw the concentration of the audience to itself. The opposite is true when a puppet bobs and wobbles about the stage with

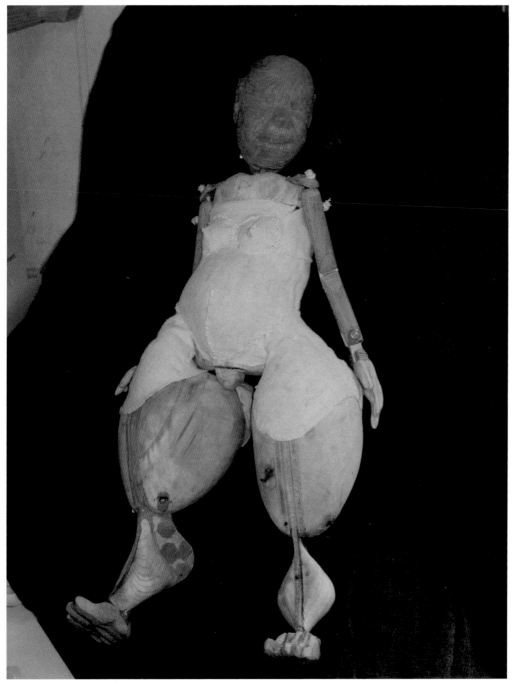

The front of the puppet.

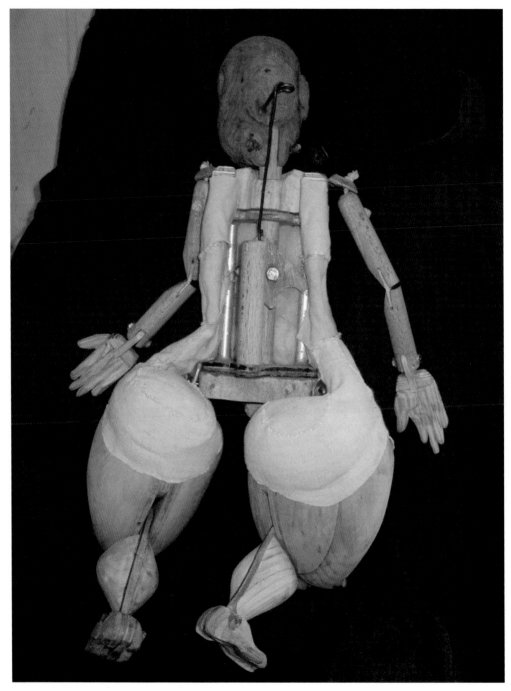

The technical reality behind its back.

The attentive puppet.

Working with a sweatshirt as a bird in rehearsal.

no particular emphasis or purpose and the audience fails to realize which are the meaningful movements and which are nothing more than a lack of stillness.

When puppet and animator are both visible onstage there needs to be a moment when the audience has time to decide which of them is supposed to draw its attention. This moment of stillness, this connection with the audience, must happen before the audience can concentrate on the ensuing action. The matter may be settled quite simply by the puppet looking at the audience and the animator looking at the puppet; it will immediately become clear whether human or object is the key player in the scene.

However skilled the operator and however beautiful and convincing the puppet, it is a lifeless bundle without character or soul if the animator does not transfer the knowledge and feeling of the character from his or her body and mind to the puppet. The puppet may perform the actions and speak the lines, but the audience won't react to it as a real character. The collective reaction may be one of delight at the puppet's beauty and astonishment at the technical expertise which went into its creation, but the audience won't love it, fear it or mind very much what happens to it.

Puppeteers may have trained in acting or dance and will have often worked with masks or the more physical forms of theatre, but the practical longing to make puppets leads them to a facility to animate their work onstage. There is no doubt that they are a particular type of performer; they are not subject to the same urge actually to appear and tell stories though their own body and voice as are actors. They seek the stage light for their puppets, not for themselves. The character they present in the course of the action will tend to be that of narrator, inventor, explainer or some other character in league with the audience, rather than a dramatic personality.

Even unpainted, Mephistopheles commands attention as he tries on his hat in the workshop of the Amsterdam Marionette Theatre.

There is no single correct way to animate puppets and objects and the people who do this extraordinary job are not cast in similar moulds. Animators' attitudes to the objects they bring to life vary from a reverent spirituality that invests the puppet with its own mystical power to an uncomplicated and matter-of-fact cheerfulness. Each may believe that his or her own methods are the only true and valid way of bringing a puppet to life, but all of them share a serious and energetic intensity which runs through their work. The work of these puppeteers divides into three fuzzy-edged categories. The divisions are not sharp or unshifting; they can overlap and change during a single performance and many practitioners work in all sorts of different ways.

STYLES OF ENGAGEMENT

The Neutral or Invisible Animator

These puppeteers perform through their puppets or objects. Whether they are visible onstage or screened from the audience, they have no interest in projecting their own personality and body. Some have a strong belief that if they were seen the audience's belief in the reality of the world of the puppet would shatter. Others assume that the audience will ignore them so long as they do not draw attention to themselves.

They often arrive at animation through the workshop that creates the puppets rather than through the stage door or through family tradition and are more at ease when performing through the puppet's body than through their own. They may have been sculptors, engineers or inventors of gadgets or stories who have needed an outlet for their ideas that was not contained within the strictures of their usual work. It is a very rare and strange job to create all these complex emotional journeys for the public without ever receiving direct contact with your audience; it calls for a balance of intellect, imagination and skill which can take years to acquire. Perhaps this type of work is closer to watching and listening than to performing.

There are practitioners who use ideas and skills born from these methods in work where the advantages of puppet performers and the lack of human boundaries and restrictions are exploited to the full. There is something about the shrinking in physical size possible in a puppet theatre that allows performance explorations into philosophy, politics or ethical complexities that might smack of the lecture room in more conventional theatre. Perhaps the fact that the audience can take in huge events in one eyeful, or that it is impossible for a puppet to be pompous, is responsible for this happy phenomenon.

When you watch one of these expert performers, the full blaze of their concentration is on the puppet or object. Their relationship to everything that is happening is through the puppet and their focus scarcely shifts to encompass changes of direction or the complex manoeuvres that may go on backstage as animators change position or exchange puppets. Their consciousness of the audience and their relation to the performance is absorbed via the puppet. It is easy to understand how in some cultures the puppets acquire a religious significance despite the prosaic business of keeping their joints oiled, their costumes clean and their strings untangled.

There are all sorts of tricks that encourage the audience to ignore the puppeteer's presence on the stage, but the most powerful is his or her concentration on the puppet, and the absence of personal involvement with the audience and with the plot. Once this has been established, the puppet is in the metaphorical, as well as the actual, spotlight. The puppet will be closer to the audience than the animator. Two puppets speaking to each other on stage will look at each other and be in the best place onstage for the audience to see them; their animators will be less well placed and less well lit.

The Double Dialogue

The concentration this demands is intense, as the puppeteer is in fact acting two parts at the same time and holding both their characters and their inner lives in their concentration.

The puppet and the animator may have a conversation with each other. The two characters they represent speak at different times, but both must remain alert and in character whilst the other is the focus of attention. Even when the puppeteer is speaking in their own character, part of their brain is concentrating on creating the reaction of the puppet to what is being said. It is difficult enough to imagine, let alone to perform. Like an iceberg, the greater part of the skill involved in this schizoid feat is hidden below the surface. Hands and voices and bodies may be performing in view of the audience, but the complex feat of imagination that keeps the hearts of the

Puppets hang in the storeroom waiting to tell their stories.

two characters alive and performing within one body is invisible.

When the animator provides both voices, the focus of attention must swing from puppet to human with the flow of the conversation. We humans, even though most of us are unlikely to be in danger of being eaten by ravening beasts, are still programmed by nature to pay attention to small movements, even when they occur on the very edge of vision. We make an instinctive assumption that the thing which looks as if it is producing the sound is really doing it. You can test this theory by listening to a miked performance with your eyes shut; it is extremely difficult to work out who's making the sound unless the voices are obviously distinctive. Or you can try to talk or sing whilst keeping completely still – it will prove to be almost impossible. We are used to seeing people move slightly when they talk and following the direction of their gaze. The puppeteer uses this sense to control the audience, who will watch the object that moves and not the thing that is still. The same technique can be reversed so that the puppet appears to control its puppeteer and turn reality on its head.

Puppet and Animator as One Character

The puppeteer can be visible and share the character with the puppet. They are one and have the same emotions. The expression of the body and face of the puppeteer will reflect that of the puppet and both puppeteer and puppet will engage with the audience. This opens the possibility of displaying an emotional state with frankness and complexity that might seem overacted with the actor performing alone. The performer could be frightened but the puppet frankly terrified; the actor politely amused while the puppet is helpless with

---

It could happen like this …

A performer may play both themself and a puppet at the same time, and be using both ways of communication at once. Imagine a girl (real actor) and her beloved dog (puppet which the same actor animates). The dog is overexcited to see the girl and wants to jump all over her and lick and romp and play. The girl is trying to make him appear calm and well-behaved. The two opposing emotions – one of abandoned joy and the other of nervous strictness – must both be played, physically and possibly verbally, by the same actress at the same time. And the audience must see and understand the points of view of both dog and girl; it must be convinced by this emotional and physical juggling. A successful result can only be achieved after much rehearsal and a complete understanding of the emotional state of both dog and girl, combined with crisp choreography of their movements. Try soothing your head with slow, calm strokes whilst thumping your stomach with frenzied anger, all the while keeping a neutral expression, if you want to gain an inkling of how difficult this is.

---

laughter. There is also a useful surprise element, perhaps comic or frightening, when a puppeteer who has been neutral unexpectedly engages directly with the audience and comments on the puppet's performance. Or vice versa.

Marionettes

The animation of any sort of puppet is a skilled and practised art, but perhaps the skill of animating a marionette takes longest to acquire. A marionette is distanced from its animator by the length of the strings. The complicated

105

It could happen like this ...

The Wolves in the Walls

The puppets are wolves. Scary, predatory and sometimes comic wolves. Their animators are dressed not to seem invisible, but in tweedy jodhpurs, sweaters and jackets which somehow suggest their human characters, plus the flanks, shins and hides of the animals they are animating. The colours they are wearing and the colours of the puppets are close in tone but there is more attention demanded by the lively way the textures and eyes of the puppets catch the stage light than the smoother textures of the actors' clothes which absorb the light. Though we see the faces and heads of the performers reflecting the emotions of the wolves, there is no sense that they are pretending to be animals, that they are separate from the wolves. It does not matter to the audience that each creature has the puppeteer's human head beside the wolf's head and its snapping fangs, or that the wolf has animal paws and human feet. Both characteristics, human and vulpine, perform together to create characters which are definitely wolves but with all the most wolfish behaviour of humans. And the audience, adults and children alike, have no difficulty in accepting these hybrid creatures as real wolves and a different species from the other humans onstage.

Wolves and their animators relax during a break in rehearsal.

For further information about Improbable and the National Theatre of Scotland's production, The Wolves in the Walls, visit www.improbable.co.uk and www.nationaltheatrescotland.com

movements of hands, arms and body can happen a long way from the puppet performing on the stage below. The words and music may be on a prerecorded soundtrack that allows for no variation in the synchronization of the puppet's actions; Don Giovanni's string may break and his lute fall lifeless from his hand, but his seductive serenade will keep going, and the puppeteer must somehow carry the action and audience through the hiatus.

The animator is looking down on the puppet from above and can feel, rather than see, when the puppet's feet are in contact with the stage floor. Unlike plays with live performers, a single role may be played by many different animators. The positioning of the puppeteers,

Two different clusters of marionette controls.
ABOVE: *the experimental build-up.*
BELOW: *the first try-out.*

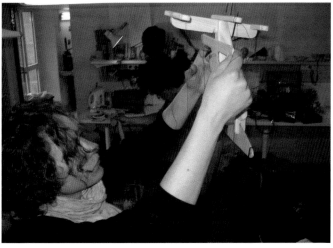

usually on a construction rather like a bridge above the stage, means that the controls may be passed from hand to hand as the puppet crosses the stage in order that the puppeteers do not have to cross and recross each other on a narrow platform. Complicated action may require more than the two controlling hands to lift and cross strings and control bars. These puppeteers are unable to see the result of their actions from the same plane and viewpoint as the audience. They have to rely on their director and the audience reaction to tell them when the marionettes below them are giving the right message. Each puppet and character has different behaviour and the movement must be learnt afresh even when the control system is familiar to the puppeteer.

Most animators of marionettes have a particular method of arrangement of crossbars and strings that suits the size, strength and flexibility of their hands. The smallest gesture, such as a tiny turn of the head created by a slight rotation of the wrist, can create a telling moment or change of mood or focus onstage; every movement of the puppeteer's hands and body must be precise and controlled.

For the first few minutes of a marionette performance the audience is conscious of the strings and the lack of reality in the walking puppet's contact with the ground. This doesn't last, as is demonstrated by the laughter that will occur when a 'human' puppet flies off the stage swung on its strings into puppet heaven; the audience is laughing at itself and at its own belief in the little figures that have worked their way into their intelligence. Despite the fact that we humans spend our lives bound by gravity, we are able to enter and accept the odd gravitational rules which, however skilled the operator, exist in the marionette world. Even the most logical human, at some time in their

life, will have dreamt of being able to fly. It takes some children a good few years before they realize they will never be able to. Perhaps an instinctive recognition of this feeling, this wish to be free from gravity, is one of the keys that makes us willing to be convinced of a most human truth emanating from these little wooden bodies on strings.

The word 'marionette' may conjure a rather simplistic clownlike or toylike figure that will perform quite simple actions to tell a simple tale. Much of its charm may lie in its childlike straightforwardness. However, there is a more serious and richer vein in their potential to perform that is used by writers and animators who have a deep message to convey. The marionette, with its somewhat surreal ability to perform at a distance from its operators while retaining the semblance of humanity, can be used as an actor in the more extreme stories of spectacle. Births, sex and deaths can occur onstage with frankness and in detail that would create a furore in commercial theatres. Scenes of graphic and horrific violence, nakedness and brutality are allowed to be shown uncensored to the public through these wooden bodies. Complex philosophical truths and ethical dichotomies can be presented with gentle insistence through their actions. Perhaps it is the fact that they do not appear to be physically connected to their operators by those fragile-seeming strings that gives puppet action an innocence in which all is allowed.

Glove Puppets

The glove puppet works in a different way from the marionette. It is far easier to manipulate the mouth of a glove puppet, usually with the thumb and finger or fingers, than to move a marionette's hinged jaw with strings and weights. The synchronization of the glove

Making a glove puppet.
RIGHT: cutting the costume.
BELOW: the finishing touches.

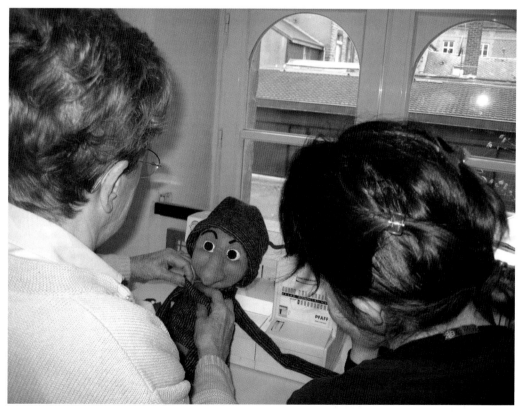

puppet's mouth movements with the words encourages the audience to be convinced that the speech is coming from its mouth. The puppeteer may be concealed, usually below the stage as in the Punch and Judy booth, with just their hands, dressed in the puppets, seen by the audience. It is a direct manner of animation. The fingers move and the puppet moves and talks. There is no distance and rarely any pretence at legs or complex body moves. A realistic physical contact between puppets is achieved; a hug is the result of two hands clasping each other inside the puppets' glove bodies and the effect of gravity is more apparent in their contact with objects. They do not bounce in strange rhythm though life as their stringed brothers and sisters often do.

When the puppeteer is in sight of the audience and they can see quite clearly that the hand of the performer is inside the puppet, new possibilities open up. Surreal and Absurdist Theatre is often discussed in academic circles as a separate and quite elitist form of theatre. But what could be more surreal and absurd, yet more familiar a sight to an audience, than an animator and their puppet having a conversation? The possibilities opened up by this form of conversation vary from the adult and bawdy humour, which reminds the audience that the puppet is performing with someone's hand stuffed up its rear end, to the innocent childishness of the mischievous glove puppet that makes fun of its animator. The content may be for two totally different types of audience, but the hub of the joke is the same, in that it relies on the ridiculousness of someone arguing with themselves and our recognition of the fact that we all have different sides to our characters. Our enjoyment is simply heightened on the occasions when the puppet seems to be winning the control battle with its animator.

Visible or Invisible?

A decision has to be made as to whether the puppeteer will be visible and how they will be dressed. Will they be all in black so that it is easy for the audience to understand that they are not supposed to include them in their understanding of the action? Will they wear hoods, so that their eyes are not visible and they become expressionless? Or will they wear costume in the same style as the puppets so that they become part of the action and are noticed by the audience?

If hoods are worn, they must be of a material thin enough to see through but thick enough to obscure the features; test this in the dimmest light that will be used during the performance and make sure they are available early enough in the rehearsal period for actors to get used to wearing them. If it is difficult to see through the cloth, a band of thinner black mesh can replace the hood cloth over the eyes. The hood should be wide enough at the shoulder point to tuck in the neck of the costume or sit over it. The easiest way to achieve this shape is for two triangular gussets of cloth to be inserted at the shoulder points.

Gloves should be of thin and clinging material, such as stretch cotton jersey with some Lycra content, so that they will not slip and do not impede the sensitivity of the hands.

Sleeves should not get in the way of manipulation and should have cuffs close to the wrist. Shoes should be non-slip and supple. If boots are worn, they should be soft enough to allow the ankles to bend freely.

THE ACTOR AS ANIMATOR

Actors present themselves onstage. They may be disguised and adopting a character far from their own, but they are looking through their own eyes at the audience and hearing with their own ears. Actors must be self-conscious to perform. They have to be certain that all eyes are drawn to them and that they are in the right place in the right light to show the way their character feels; they must also react, still in sight of the audience, with the other actors onstage. The way their costume looks and feels on their body, their make-up and their posture all give a feeling of stability to the role they are playing.

The puppet is selfless and breathes only with the help of its animator. The actor must discard the stability of his or her own body and learn to look through the puppet's eyes, hear through its ears and breathe for it. The audience's attention must be channelled away from the actor towards the puppet. Actors have the advantage of a training, interest and experience in finding an echo in themselves of a character they are playing and bringing it into the open air of performance. The actor can believe in, and in a way become, another person. It is one step further in the process to send this belief down your arm and into an inanimate object in order to make it, not yourself, the star of the show. It requires a rearrangement of many of your instincts as a performer.

Daring to Animate

Actors are used to manipulating props and rarely worry about manipulating objects, which they can settle in the same category as props. Nevertheless, the first response of many actors when asked to animate a puppet in rehearsal is to back away and suggest employing an experienced puppeteer for the job. This hurdle has to be jumped by the actor, director and puppet maker before rehearsals start being productive.

It helps if the puppet designer/maker is there, with the puppets, for the first read-through and rehearsal. Their presence, even with the puppets in an unfinished state, will be invaluable. The director and designer/maker can then introduce the actors to the puppets and the company can start to play and experiment rather than theorize. The pressure of this first rehearsal will be relaxed if everyone takes a turn playing with each puppet, and not only the ones will they be animating in performance. Inexperienced puppeteers may find it helpful if the company builds up a collection of movements for each puppet that will form the basis of the movements to be used for that puppet's moods and actions. The collection will be refined and improved later on as confidence and ability grow, but will provide a practical and visible base to build on.

Shifting the Focus

Actors are used to knowing how they look on stage. They develop an instinct which tells them how to present themselves to the audience and they learn techniques of movement which would often be unnatural in real life but appear natural on a stage. Most of these are designed to open out the action to the audience's perception; if two actors clasp hands with their downstage hands (those nearest the audience) the most expressive areas of their bodies will be turned away from the audience, whereas clasping upstage hands opens and exposes the body and its language. There are all sorts of tricks, turns and positions which actors use to give the audience a clear view of the onstage action. They know how to find the light that exposes them most clearly and the angles that reveal their expressions; without this, the audience would be deprived of great parts of understanding of the emotional state

111

Shifting the focus. Puppeteer Lee Threadgold shifts the puppet's focus to himself ...

... and to another character on stage ...

... but his own focus stays on the puppet.

of the character. Many of these stock-in-trade acting techniques will be reversed when animating puppets and that can be a difficult process.

The Mirror and the Outside Eye

Most makers and animators of puppets and objects work with a mirror in the workroom or rehearsal room. There are problems to this as the viewpoint is reversed; if you move the puppet's hand to the right the mirror hand moves to the left. You are not looking from the same angle as the audience. The greatest drawback is that you cannot look at the reflection in the mirror and put all your concentration into projecting life into the puppet. But it's a useful practical aid to establishing which gestures and actions work well from the point of view of the audience, and to teach yourself the hand and body movements that create those gestures.

There are many cases when an animator has to rely on the outside eye of a director or colleague to tell them what works. In such cases, the gestures that create a telling movement have to be learnt as a technical exercise. It helps, in such cases, if someone else takes over the animation of the puppet for a rehearsal, so that the actual animator can see from a seat in the auditorium the effect that is created by the gestures.

TRANSFORMING OBJECTS

Animators of Objects

Animators of objects have an equal number of variations and complications, though it's unusual for them to immerse themselves into the character of the object in the same way as they might with a puppet. This is because the object never loses its inanimate status the way puppet characters do when they start performing. Members of the audience still hold in the back of their minds the knowledge that they are conniving with the performers to allow the objects their power onstage; it's a bit like sharing a joke, or the message in an exchanged glance which draws people together in understanding. The performers use this collusion with the audience to tumble the barrier between the stage and the stalls and to create a more intense and inclusive experience for everyone, without the more aggressive moments of audience participation which can alienate as often as they include.

Investigating Objects

Objects can produce an inner life if they are given the chance. It's a meditative business and not to be hurried. We are used to handling the objects of our everyday life with a careless familiarity; after all, we've become familiar with the way they feel and the work they are used for since we first touched them. Exploring these objects with a concentrated sense of discovery renews in us the recognition of the nature within the objects. It is very hard to talk about stuff like this without sounding weird and a bit transcendental. It is neither. It's just looking at and feeling stuff without prejudice. Pick up any object you use every day. Your pencil or your mug, your spectacles or a shoe. Pick it up without thinking. You will find you handle it with a familiar consciousness of its use, and your hands will make their habitual adjustments that prepare for the action that usually follows. You may pick up your pencil and adjust your grip as if you were going to take off its top, or poise it to write. Pick up your shoe and you will automatically prepare to put it on your foot or position it in the shoe rack.

But then pick up the mug or the spectacles as if you had never seen them before and didn't know what they were or what they might do. They adopt a new significance. Their weight, their sound, the way they reflect light, their colour and the way they can move in the air or on a surface can produce a whole new scope of interest. It may sound daft, but try it and see. This exploration is one of the paths into working with objects in performance.

It is quite possible that one of these objects, whose purpose is so well known to you, will reveal a surprising side of its character and set you off on a train of invention. Pick up the pencil again and make it cover some ground on paper. Held firmly and vertically, it might march in a regular sequence of dashes across the page; hold it gently and tipped to one side and it may make a series of seductive curves. Holding the pencil in strict marching position while creating the same waltzing curves, or making it quick-march in a gentle hand feels unnatural. Sounds you make to accompany the pencil's journey will follow the dictates of the character the pencil has become. The mood of the grip and the object have fused; the pencil has become both an inspiration and a performer. Don't be misled into thinking that

Actors play with simple objects in rehearsal.

an audience will see what you see in this exploration, or necessarily be as interested in the object's hidden powers as you are. It may be fascinating to watch, but then so is any demonstration that engrosses the whole concentration of its perpetrator. But it is not a performance. It is merely an experiment in a new way of enjoying objects, a way of playing that will be useful as one of the tools in a particular sort of theatre.

Making Objects for Performance

Some of these experiments will result in props that will be used in the show. The experiments that actors work with will have to be recreated to function in a practical way, performance after performance. The object used in rehearsal, when everybody knows what they want to see and what they are trying to achieve, may be impractical, impenetrable and too breakable to be a reliable prop. It may be too small, or the wrong colour or texture to show up onstage. The audience will be seeing all these things for the first time, amid other objects and distractions with which they are unfamiliar. The rehearsal object may have to be adapted, strengthened and presented to give the public every chance to enjoy the same exciting moment of invention that occurred in the rehearsal room at the moment of its creation.

At this point, the director and designer/maker must stand back from their knowledge of the rehearsed events and put themselves in the audience's shoes, envisaging the event as a new experience. A decision must be made as to the exact function of the object so that it can be made to fit the purpose. It is crucial to position the object to give the audience the best view and to light it to its best advantage. The sound that accompanies the action must be

It could happen like this ...

The narrative demands that a battalion of infantry marches to the battlefield. The soldiers are highly trained, obedient and pitiless. Circumstances demand that one man must play the whole battalion. The exercise with the marching pencil gives the idea for a battalion of sticks mounted like bristles on a platform that can be moved by one person on the same principle as a wheelbarrow.

The regular jerking motion of the march is produced by using a hexagonal rather than a circular wheel at the front of the contraption. The audience is certain that it is seeing a fighting force because of the military march that accompanies the battalion's progress; the audience's certainty could be reinforced, if it was felt to be necessary, by giving the sticks helmets, or by using rifles instead of sticks. If the wheel was round, the music holy and the sticks black and white lilies, the now smooth-running contraption could become a group of nuns processing to worship. Of course, it would be possible to use the same effect with fully costumed dummies, but it would not necessarily convey a more believable picture of the event; it would depend on the context and genre of the piece and would eat a bigger slice of the budget.

composed and the actors must rehearse the sequence until the whole effect is seamless and certain.

The Role of the Audience

When choosing objects for performance this experiment reverses from being an internalized game to one that involves the audience through its inclusion in a play. The play may have a tight narrative drive or may have a

Thanks to a false bottom in the box, the actor vanishes into his coffin in a shower of black polythene rain. Photo: Alistair Milne

looser, abstract content more related to dance or a piece of music. The objects used in the piece must have a reason to be there other than as a display of clever invention. Often in the more abstract work it is the recognition of the way that a familiar object can change its purpose and meaning that delights members of the audience, leading their imaginations into a world where anything is possible and nothing is what it seems.

These objects give actors, and their directors and designers, a chance to show the audience how much it is trusted to support and collude in the performance onstage and how necessary its involvement is to the success of the work. You can't pretend a suitcase can eat a man unless you believe your audience will play too, and the audience, when this trust is displayed so blatantly, responds with its best and most imaginative involvement with the happenings onstage.

You can feel the evidence of this particular, all-inclusive comradeship between actors and audience in the friendliness of the applause at the end of the show. It seems as right for the actors to applaud the audience for its creative input as for the public to applaud its actors.

9. WORK FOR CHILDREN

A well-behaved lamb made of shredded paper and old tights.

A long tradition of puppet theatre work has left us with the rather cosy Victorian or 1950s image of children sitting in rows watching fairly undemanding stuff. This was never true.

There have always been people telling stories that demanded more of their young audience than polite attention. But today, work for children, while still respecting the traditional stories, themes and techniques, includes some of the most innovative and imaginative puppet and object work in performance today.

Practitioners who work for an audience of children have access to information no adult audience will give them. Children show what they feel about the work, honestly and clearly. If it works they are engaged, concerned and controlled, but if they are not interested they make it perfectly clear that they would rather be doing something else.

The phrases 'object theatre' and 'visual theatre' are unfamiliar to people who are not regular theatre-goers. The phrase 'puppet theatre' is often assumed to mean 'puppet theatre for children'. The reality – a growth of the use of objects and puppets in mainstream adult theatre – is beginning to change this assumption. Children may have less experience with words than adults, but they are better at decoding the world through gesture, tone, rhythm and body-language. They have fewer preconceptions about theatrical experience. They are closer to the sort of play that gives life to inanimate objects and to a world where you do not need words to explain things. They do not have to be cajoled, as adults do, to play along with the company, though they may take a bit more persuading as they get older.

Object and visual theatre creates work that the whole family can enjoy together, a situation that has for many years been the province of pantomime and musicals. Theatre made specifically for young children prepares this audience for a rewarding theatre-going future. The content and style of all this work is as varied as that of adult theatre. The surreal nature of performing objects, the intelligent, creative content of the work and the demands it makes of its audience are accepted without question by children as long as the character and heart of the performance is true.

AUDIENCE PARTICIPATION

Theatre gives children a chance to be on an equal footing with adults and influence the behaviour of the world. Their participation in the direction the story takes onstage gives them an experience they cannot get any other way. Television and films can't provide it; everything has been sorted out in advance for them. Stories are wonderful, but the book is written and children's imaginations are engaged in interpreting rather than influencing the story.

The full-throated roar of support from a young audience is one of the most exciting sounds anyone ever hears in a theatre, equalled only by the held-breath silence of their interest and suspense.

Repetition
Moments of repetition within the script delight a young child. These moments put them in control of the proceedings and allow them to change the focus of their concentration to a more active participation, particularly if they have the opportunity to join in and apparently influence the happenings onstage. They can help influence the action, warn about impending danger or make magic. These opportunities will be balanced by some device within the story that will control the eagerness of the children when it might prevent the continuation of the play. If the story asks the children to make waves and wind to help drive the boat to the shore by whooshing the wind and waving their arms to make the movement of the sea, they will stop without being asked when they see that the boat has reached the shore and all

is well. They will also start again with the slightest hint if the boat is in trouble again.

These moments do not come about automatically. They are the result of imagination, planning and rehearsal. The practitioners who are best at it trust the children to work with them. They make work which would be incomplete without the children's participation. Instructions, even when they are disguised by the action, need to be clear so that all the children, not just the more confident ones, are certain that they are being asked for their help and how the help is to be given.

CONTENT

The subject matter of the work must be appropriate to the understanding of the child.

This is not as limiting as it sounds; the same subject can form the basis of a story for all ages but the slant must be appropriate and must respect the child's development. A theme of homelessness could be about a lost mouse's adventures as he searches the forest for his home, or the journey of a teenage rebel from their home to a cardboard city full of drugs and danger.

Performance for Babies and Toddlers

Very young children don't play by the rules in theatres. They don't know them and there is no reason why they should. A baby or toddler can enjoy a performance very much indeed, but, unless they are physically retrained by their parents or scared, they will see no reason why they should not climb onto the stage with the performers, play with the puppets and chew the objects. They want to touch and play. If they like the music they will dance. If they like the way an object moves they will want to try it out for themselves. If they like the actors

they will want to get close to them and cuddle or sit on them. The most successful work for this youngest audience allows them to explore it for themselves.

A stage and an auditorium is a difficult venue to arrange for this to happen safely. The health and safety hazard of a crowd of children pursued by their parents scrambling around a theatre would give any production or stage manager nightmares. You cannot have a large audience consisting only of very young children as each one will be accompanied by at least one adult and perhaps their older siblings. The venue must be safe and the floor clean.

Words are not particularly important to this age group, though sound is; their language is touch and texture, smell and colour and movement. This means that puppets and objects used for such performance cannot be like the usual theatre stuff. Objects and the set must be strong enough to cope with being tugged, chewed, chucked and climbed over. They must be washable and waterproof so that the paint doesn't come off when it's wet. Detail can be simple. A very young baby will understand that two eyes painted on a ball are a person. The director/inventor of the work and the performers make it a performance and an early experience of theatre rather than a nursery. They give character as well as movement to the puppets and objects. They create a structure which may be as simple as the audience following the bouncing eyes-on-a-ball character through a series of situations, but that everyone, actors and audience, experience together.

School-Age Children

Children under twelve want stories. Puppet and object theatre work often proves to offer

A wizard and the narrator/animator – so obviously from different species.

the widest, most adaptable environment for presenting these stories. Anything is possible for puppets. Witches and animals, fairies, giants, robots and the fantastic cast that has always absorbed children's interest can inhabit puppets and so be freed from the bodies that tie humans to reality. The ease with which children can imagine life into inanimate objects makes object theatre a natural way to tell the story. The method can be free even when the story is precise.

Comedy

The things children find funny are not always the same as the things that make adults roar with laughter. Children love repetition. A character accidentally treads in a bucket and hops around with the bucket stuck on his foot. The children find it hilarious. The actor does it again; they still find it very, very funny. And again. And again. And again. The anticipation and the certainty of what is about to happen as the character approaches the bucket make the joke even better; the actor will get bored long before the children do, and the adults in the audience, though they may enjoy the sight and sound of the riotous laughter, will not be particularly amused after the second or third time. Adults are used to knowing the result of actions. Young children are not. Their worlds

Julian Crouch's wolf, the children's enemy, hits the balance between terror and comedy...

... while Jade and Jack stay on more familiar territory.

are full of actions which produce results that are a total surprise; think of the pleasure a young child gets from stamping in a puddle and seeing the splash, and how long they can go on doing it without getting bored. It is a great pleasure for children to be able to anticipate the punchline, or in this case the punch-bucket, of a joke. Particularly when the butt of the joke is an adult.

Fear

It is a responsible task to make work for children. The material and presentation must be appropriate to the age and experience of the audience. Fear has to be respected. A young child may be terrified by sudden darkness, crashing sound and above all frightening creatures onstage; they have no reason to believe

that the monster will stay on stage and not come out into the audience and really gobble them up. The worlds of reality, theatre and dreams have no distinct boundaries. Fear may make them incapable of enjoyment and interest. An eight- or nine-year-old has a different attitude. They have seen more life, with the result that the frisson of fear adds a thrill to their enjoyment and sharpens their concentration and involvement in the performance. They understand the difference between imagination and reality, and have the mental maturity to know that the evil will stay onstage and that it is their own mind that allows it to come into the audience.

The barrier between imagination and reality remains wobbly and of variable thickness. It grows slowly and depends on the nature of each person. A scriptwriter or director for the primary school age group has to allow for the possibility that, while some children have this barrier under control, for others it is a penetrable mist that allows nightmares into real life.

Morals and Ethics

The five-year-old may be only just beginning to understand that there is grey ground between black and white; that good and bad can intermingle and are not set at opposite ends of the spectrum. The world is painted in broad strokes. A ten-year-old will understand; they will most likely have had quite complex brushes with this grey ground and will be interested in exploring it. Older children want to engage with subject matter that concerns the lives of their age group. The maker of children's drama has the opportunity of influencing an exploration of right and wrong, as well as the more difficult issues that children battle with in their daily life. Puppets provide an opening to have characters on stage that would perhaps be unacceptable in the performance of a live actor. You might not, for instance, want to see a genuinely fat and bespectacled real-life boy being tormented by a group of children onstage, but using puppets to explore the damage of bullying could be

A puppet whose tongue is cut out (by means of a magnet) to prevent her incriminating her attacker, made for the more adult teenage audience.

123

presented without the same uneasy connotations and with as much power.

Teenage Children

Teenage children make a demanding, questioning public and you have to win their trust. They are conscious of the way they seem to other members of the audience and it takes longer for them to forget themselves and become engrossed in a story. Puppets offer them a way to explore issues that concern them, as long as any preconceptions they have about puppets being childish are overcome. The best way to do this is to surprise them or make them laugh. Objects, which have such power to surprise and transform, creep in under the defence. Puppets that are made in an unfamiliar way will do the same thing. A teenage rebel character made as a beautiful marionette may not make the same immediate connection with the teenage audience as an animated hoody/sweatshirt with an i-pod. The combination of a serious issue which concerns their age group, such as interracial problems or peer pressure, and an unexpected transformation of the objects of a classroom into the dramatis personae of a story, might set up a climate of comedy and serious debate on which to build the performance. After-show discussions with this age group are particularly rewarding.

PERFORMANCE

Rehearsals

Work that leaves space for the participation of the audience has a bit of a problem in rehearsal because that vital ingredient is missing. The director and actors have to guess what will happen, and though the presence of

---

It could happen like this ...

In *Midnight*, a stage adaptation by Vicky Ireland of the Jacqueline Wilson story, the fairy world and the human world exist side by side, though the audience and the heroine are the only ones who can see the fairies. There is a problem with fairies onstage; they are smaller than humans and they can fly. Neither of these two inhibiting factors is a problem for puppets. These *Midnight* fairies were small and detailed with strange twig-like hands and delicate, expressive faces. They inhabited a world divorced from gravity and solidity. They could fly and hover. The delicate hands could make precise gestures. Their clothes floated with their movement and the fabrics of their costumes caught the stage light in a way that made it appear that even the light they flew in was of an unearthly quality. They were rod puppets, and their animators controlled the precise movement of the heads with one rod and the hand with another, thinner rod. The puppeteers, although quite visible to the audience, appeared unimportant and in no way diminished the impression of scale. Actors could not have played those fairies. The juxtaposition of the puppets with the human characters made the contrast of the two worlds even more apparent.

The puppets in Vicky Ireland's adaptation of Jacqueline Wilson's Midnight *were designed by Gemma Fripp and made by Lee Threadgold. For further information about this production, visit www.watershedtheatre.com and www.sjt.uk.com*

---

any of the company filling in for the children is useful, it gives an insubstantial guide to what will happen when the children are actually there. This means that the first performances in front of an audience become part of the rehearsal process. Changes, sometimes as slight as the tilt of a puppet's head to invite comment from the children, or more complex, such as discovering a way to call a halt to the children's enthusiastic input without actually asking them to be quiet and sit down, have to be re-rehearsed. Everyone, backstage, onstage and front of house, learns to be ready to change and react to whatever happens when the work and the children meet.

Foyer and Auditorium

For many children the show may be their first experience of live performance and the first time they have been inside a theatre building.

That experience is more than just the show. It starts when they come into the building: the out-of-the-ordinary occasion; the crowd in the foyer; the pictures and perhaps puppets on display; the tickets and the seats are all part of the experience. The children may not know that they are expected to sit down and listen, or they may have been told to sit quietly and then have to be persuaded to participate. Any performance for children is likely to have a wide age range in the audience; the show may be aimed at six- to ten-year-olds but there will be younger brothers and sisters and, of course, parents. Work that is good is rarely boring to anyone, even if the content is too young or too old for some sections of the audience – they

Children watch for the puppets to come out of their box. Photo: Mar Mateo

will all enjoy it in different ways. Younger children will comment and question during the show. Adults will enjoy the reactions of the children as much as the story.

After the Show

Some people think the magic is destroyed if puppets are shown without animation, but everyone, child or adult, loves the opportunity to get a closer look after the show at the things they have seen onstage. It is not always practical to let children handle the objects, but it is good if there are as many people as possible to answer questions and show and tell the children what they want to know; the technical aspects of the show will interest most children as much as the content. They want to know how things work. Most don't have any prob-

lem with knowing the real facts and allowing the imaginary ones to exist side by side, or in editing out facts which interfere with the way they want to enjoy the show. Children are quite capable of watching a puppet or object being animated by a visible puppeteer and asking where the batteries are that make it move.

It can be confusing for actors to work in front of a silent audience. It is easy to make children laugh, shout and run around and bang the interesting flap of a theatre seat up and down. But the rapt involvement of a child in the story unfolding on stage, the concentrated gaze of all those eyes on the action and a silence as deep as that in a concert hall full of avid Bach enthusiasts, is the greatest compliment a young audience can pay to the company.

10. Puppets and Objects in the Community, Teaching and Therapy

STREET THEATRE

The age-old tradition of the travelling player roaming the world continues to bring theatre and spectacle to places and people who might never see any other sort of performance in their lifetime. On its travels through the latter years of the twentieth century and early twenty-first, this work gained new impetus. People had become used to watching television as a daily part of their lives. They had become accustomed to seeing performances on screen in two dimensions, then re-forming them in their imaginations to a three-dimensional reality. For a little while, it seemed as if all sorts of theatre would founder on the rocks of these enticing and accessible screens. But gradually live performance, which uses audience imagination in such a different manner, righted itself and carried on sailing. Live street performance has gathered new ideas, techniques and equipment and added them to the traditional repertoires. A remote-controlled puppet with a belly full of precise engineering might seem a long way from a glove puppet made from an old sock, but both are absorbed by the work on the street and by the attention of the audience.

Wherever there is a tradition of street theatre there will be puppets. It's a democratic business. The audience is not an informed theatre-going public. Anybody and everybody sees it and watches it, not in the controlled environment of a theatre, but in a hubbub of children and bicycles, hamburger vans and traffic noise. Nobody expects to have to be quiet or still. Often they have to choose to follow or find the performers. The numbers of the audience can never be anticipated with any exactitude and the performers and performances are as varied as the audience.

Puppet performance and the work of companies who use objects or shadows to help tell a story trust the audience to follow not only the journey of the performance, but to believe that the objects that are moved around possess a life of their own. Many of these companies and artists work with puppets to create street theatre performances. The fact that the animators and manipulators are in full view and perhaps within touching distance seems to have no effect on the ability of the audience to believe in the life and soul of the objects, or in their magical properties.

The scale of the puppets used in street festivals may vary from the miniature to the gigantic. The tiny stages, where a man is the size of a finger, and the huge ones, where streets and town squares become stages for creatures the height of a three-storey house,

The audience arrives at the Electric Theatre's tiny theatre of insects. Photo: Langemeijer

share a magical skill; they turn the ordinary towns where humans live their ordinary lives into extraordinary places. They transform familiar spaces.

Who can look at a street in the same way when a creature the height of a three-storey house has paced past its shop fronts? Or who would not be fascinated by the full-scale emotions experienced by a family small enough to live in a shoebox?

PRACTICALITIES

Choosing the Spot
Street performers may be booked and paid by a festival and allotted a pitch. Choosing your own place to pitch your show depends on practical factors. You need a space away from a busy thoroughfare to perform but one where there will be passers-by to be attracted to your show. A quiet small-scale show which attracts its audience by arousing their curiosity will lose its public to a loud ebullient one that uses a strident 'Roll up! Roll up!' technique to pull the crowd. Shops will get annoyed if you block or hide their entrance and lessen their chance of customers. If the weather looks threatening or is very sunny, any sort of shelter or shade will be good. Some performances move along and perform either whilst moving, or stop, perform and then move on to the next spot, gathering a crowd along the way.

It could happen like this ...

Melodious Monk is in his basket. He is shy of the crowd and does not want to play his barrel organ for them. He's lifted out of his basket, is taken to sniff the crowd and he starts to become confident and excited. We can see he is held and animated by his puppeteer. He relaxes, greets and plays with the crowd, and begins to get a bit rowdy and out of hand. His puppeteer tries to shut him up but he ignores her. She gives him to someone in the audience to hold while she is busy at the other side of the playing space. He begins to move, to look round the crowd, to steal the suitcase of bananas. The children are not surprised; they are delighted to play with him. The adults are astonished. At last he agrees to sit down and play his music to the crowd, to bow to their applause and take round the hat for the money. But by now he is overexcited and won't stop playing. He is bribed with a banana to get back in his basket while his puppeteer clears away his little chair, his barrel organ and the rest of the props. But Monk is not inanimate in his basket. He eats the banana, he shifts around and his eyes follow the crowd. His furry little body hides a miracle of engineering that bewilders the senses. The audience sees a puppet. They see his puppeteer. But then he starts acting without her. How is it possible? They wonder if he is a real monkey pretending to be a puppet or whether they have imagined that he can move alone.

Anonymous in the audience is his second animator operating the controls hidden in his pocket. For Monk is a robot.

For more information about Electric Circus with Mirjam Langemeijer and Fred Abel's street performance puppets, visit http://compagniededraak.com/projecten.html

Gathering and Controlling the Crowd

Any sort of sound, musical or vocal, a blast or two on a horn, a bright or strange costume, or an unusual prop will encourage a crowd to gather. A small crowd will attract a larger one as people stop to see what the fuss is about. You would see a pattern to the way crowds collect round an event if you looked from above. Five is the magic number. Once five people are watching more come and form a semi-circle. When people find it impossible to see over each other's heads they spread round until the circle surrounds the player. Children wriggle to the front. The crowd regulates its own size because when people can't see they move away. The taller the performer, the bigger the crowd.

A puppet can encourage the support of the crowd with cheeky, bizarre or over-friendly behaviour that would be outrageous in a human; it can give a stranger a voluptuous kiss, or even expose himself without being arrested. Personal remarks such as 'baldy' or 'luscious lips' raise more laughs than eyebrows. Having gathered a circle, and aroused interest, the more rehearsed interplay between crowd and audience can begin. There will be people who want to get too close and become performers rather than audience. They are best controlled by being used as such. Street theatre needs involvement from the audience and the more that can be absorbed into the performance the better. The puppet can

Birds draw the crowd to the site of the performance. Photo: Brigitte Lambert

answer the hecklers, or a conspiratorial 'shhh' to a child from the animator or puppet will work better and disturb the performance far less than asking the parent to control the child.

Creating a Stage

The smallest-sized performance, even a flea circus, needs space around it so that the audience can see what is going on and the performer can feel confident in their space. A single performer and puppet will automatically clear a space around themselves; the audience acknowledges the invisible boundary surrounding the action and stays behind it, sensing that it must not get too close or the magic will be destroyed.

If this boundary is not observed, it may be reinforced by the performer in a number of ways. A playing space can be made. It may not look like a stage or even a clearing. A chalked line on the pavement or a rope lying on the ground could draw the boundary. The performer could run round the circle, suggesting with outstretched arms that the audience give space. A cloth or mat could delineate the playing area. A tape or ribbon, held at its corners by helpers or the audience, make a triangle, rectangle or square. The benefit of this system is that the helpers can shift the stage along the route by 'walking' the playing area along the route; nothing actually holds the crowd back, but the suggestion is made of audience space and playing space. It is amazing, really, how obedient the audience will be to these or any other directives. A more physical performance will make the audience sort out its own space as long as what's coming is visible far enough in advance.

Problems in the Street

Street performers have to cope with problems that do not occur in the more controlled performance space. Crowd attitude to these shows, large and small, is not the same as that of audience members who have bought tickets, perhaps organized a babysitter or dinner, put on their best clothes and gone out for an evening's entertainment. That audience will have a reasonably clear idea of what it is going to see, while the performers will have a rough notion of the sort of audience they can expect. Street theatre can spring surprises on both parties.

Puppets may be quite small and crowds quite large. The performer animating a small puppet can at least move about carrying their equipment without too many prior arrangements. Large-scale events may need traffic to be stopped or diverted, police and ambulance support to be in place and space to be cleared. This cannot be organized in a moment; plans for the route, size of the objects, crowd safety, transport and timings must all be in place perhaps months before the event. Street theatre performers, when inventing and rehearsing their work, must always keep a clear eye on practical as well as the artistic considerations. A festival will have much of the organization in place, but there will always be some questions for the individual to consider:

- Is it physically possible for the performer to manage to carry the equipment if necessary?
- Will it take too long to prepare or dismantle the equipment?
- How much help do the performers need to take with them and how much can they rely on the audience to rally round?
- Do the objects have enough room to manoeuvre in the streets?
- Are there kerbs or humps that would be obstructive to objects supported on wheels?

- Do the onlookers have space to see and follow the procession without funnelling into the possible danger of a bottleneck?
- Will the arriving people be able to locate a moving procession? The noise of a band is a most useful solution to this problem as a group of people always seek for and follow the sound of music.
- Where will these crowds find enough toilets and refreshments?
- How will the space be cleared in case of emergency?

Big events need large, professional teams to cope with all the complications that arise when there is a dramatic change in the way a public space is used. A single player may need a licence to perform in the street.

Collecting the Money

Performers need to eat and live and they expect to be paid for their work. Performers can be booked and paid for by the festival organization, although street festivals are more common in other countries of Europe than in Great Britain. The street performer who sets up a moving stage and walks with his puppet around a venue may have to collect from the audience at the end of each show. This is a skill in its own right, as the audience members can choose whether they pay or not. They do not have to stay for the collection at the end of the show and there is no set price for tickets. It is easy for people, who may have seen and enjoyed the show, to walk straight past the hat or bucket on the ground. It is less easy to resist the artist you have just seen perform looking you in the eye and holding out a bucket or passing the traditional hat. It's even harder for the most miserly scrounger to watch the show and sneak off if they have a puppet calling them names and trying to nick their wallet whilst the crowd roars with laughter.

Coping with the Elements: Wind

The south of France may have a reliable record where the weather is concerned but the south of England certainly does not. The elements, particularly in the less temperate areas, can be challenging, and though an audience will disperse if it begins to get wet rather than damp, there are other problems to contend with.

The force of the wind can cause a large puppet to behave like a sail or a kite or a flag and become uncontrollable. Think how difficult it can be to keep control of an umbrella on a gusty day and how often the whole thing, metal spokes and all, is turned inside-out by the wind. The risk of this happening can be minimized by making it possible for the wind to pass through the puppet and continue on its way without interruption. The alternatives are to make the puppet heavy enough to resist the wind, although this may also make it too heavy to manipulate easily. It may be appropriate to design the object so that the fluttering is incorporated into the design, although in that case the fabric must be light enough to retain its character whether fluttering in the breeze or static and becalmed. If you know the venue you can judge the possible risks. A windmill on a hill is bound to be windier than a town street. But even in an urban setting there can be dramatic crosswinds at road intersections or whipping round the corners of buildings. In some cases, it may be helpful to weight the feet and legs to make a more stable figure. Any form of mesh used in the construction will help to minimize the wind resistance.

Rain

Every animator who has worked out of doors has experienced the difficulties of working with a wet puppet and the difficulty of getting them dry before the next performance. The most immediate disadvantage is the extra weight. Water is heavy and an absorbent cloth, such as washed linen or thick cotton, can absorb many times its own weight in water. The wet cloth tends to stick to other wet cloth and the working joints become less mobile.

A lot depends on the fabric. Most man-made fibres are less absorbent than natural ones. Leather staves off the wet and even a small percentage of Lycra or Elastane in a fabric makes it much less absorbent. There is a spray, normally used to waterproof shoes and rain-wear, which will cause the surface of the cloth to reject liquid. As a general rule, thick, natural fibres absorb most and thin man-made fibres the least. It is worth holding a fabric up to the light to check the density of the weave; tightly woven fabric that you cannot see the light through, such as poplin, has much more fibre per square centimetre to retain the water than a loosely woven fabric such as muslin.

When hanging an object to dry, spread it so that the largest area of cloth is nearest the bottom, which will give gravity a chance to help with the dripping as well as exposing as much of the surface area as possible to the air. In an emergency, anything that creates a warm current of air – a hairdryer, a blow heater or even a hand drier in the washroom – will speed up the drying process. Circular hangers with clothes pegs attached in a wide-spaced circle to a hoop are excellent for holding the drying puppet well spaced to take advantage of any air current.

The best defence against the unruly elements is to be prepared and to imagine how the objects will react in the most adverse circumstances and to design and make with the worst scenario in mind.

WORKSHOPS IN THE COMMUNITY

People have fun making things. They also have fun performing. Work that uses puppets and objects is even more fun because you can do both at the same time. There is no age limit to this enjoyment, although it might be harder to persuade a teenager that they can engage with this style of work. There is a great satisfaction in making something with your own hands and it is important, when planning work of this kind, that something tangible is achieved by everyone by the end of the sessions. Ending the work with a performance, even if it is as simple as showing your work to other members of the group, provides a natural and satisfying goal for everyone. If the work is to end in a more public performance, a way must be found to structure the objects so that they do not appear to be the work of lots of different people with varied ideas and skills.

Although the content of the workshop may be different for different ages and groups, there can be a regular form to the way the workshops are structured.

Story and Stimuli

Inexperienced makers of puppets and objects need a stimulus to spark their imaginations. It is not that they do not have ideas. But is difficult for even an experienced inventor to pluck a thought from the air and make it solid reality, and much more difficult for someone who does not have confidence in their ability to invent and make. The stimulus makes people feel safe and gives them a goal to aim towards. When people feel safe and confident their imaginations are better and bolder.

Familiar stories are good, particularly when making puppets, unless you have time to

A puppet drying on a hoop of pegs.

Puppets made by a mixed-ability group. ABOVE: *the examples of simple card puppets.* RIGHT: *the puppets made by the group wait to begin their show.*

The children of Newham try out the bones of the dragon they are making at an 'Artburst' workshop. Photo: Amy Bicât

create a story with the group. Fairy stories, fables and myths have clear-cut characters and universal emotional and moral dilemmas. They can be childlike or adult to suit the group and most people will know these characters already, which saves time. The workshop may have been arranged to provide work that will be used in a particular procession or performance, and in that case the more people understand the nature of the rest of the show, the more they will create work which will suit the occasion.

The stimulus does not need to have a narrative drive. A more open subject, such as a confrontation or a place, perhaps under the sea or in the park, can work as the starting point for a workshop. It is also possible to use the materials themselves as stimuli, although they need to be limited and straightforward for a first attempt; newspaper and masking tape perhaps, or rubber bands and polythene bags. While this might begin as an exercise in puppeteering, it will soon develop into puppet making as people fashion the paper and polythene into more structured and easy to manoeuvre shapes.

It could happen like this ...

A group of young adults was rehearsing a play. During the action, one of the characters described a tragedy that happened to a band in which he played the trumpet. The director suggested that this trumpeter-survivor should use puppets to recreate the terrible event. The rest of the cast would create and animate the other puppet members of the band. The puppets would appear to the audience to be sticks of dynamite until their nature was revealed. Time was short and there was not much money.

In rehearsal, the actors used mineral water bottles to represent their puppets. When they arrived in the workshop to make the real ones there were several boxes of equipment for them to use:

- cardboard rolls, the sort that cloth is rolled round, sawn into lengths of between 25–35cm (10–14in)
- cardboard and small flat sticks
- scraps of cloth linked by homespun texture and earthy colours
- white and ochre paint and thick black marker pens
- glue, masking tape, rubber bands and pins to hold things in place whilst the glue dries.

The actors were free to create the particular character of their member of the band but could use only the supplies on the table. The limited range of colour and cloth, the set length of the cardboard rolls and the simplicity of the equipment ensured a similar feeling and scale for all the puppets, but allowed their creators scope for their own imaginations. The band music played in the background. As the actors sat round the table cutting and gluing their puppets, they talked. They talked about the characters developing in the cardboard, about the instruments their characters played, their relationships with each other. Conversations began between puppets. The making process turned into sort of rehearsal that grew with the puppets. When it came to the first actual rehearsal, the actors were familiar with the lives and attitudes of their puppets, their relationships to each other and the instruments they played in a way that could not have happened if they had nor made the puppets themselves.

These students were working towards a performance of The Suicide. *For further information about Performance Studies at St Mary's University College, Twickenham, visit www.smuc.ac.uk/Courses/Undergraduate/index*

Physical and Vocal Games

There would be no advantage in separating the puppet making from the puppet animation. Nobody can make a puppet without finding out how it works, and you can't find anything out without playing; you don't have to be particularly good at performing to learn a great deal about the possibilities of character and performance in your puppet. It works well, if working with children on a story, to read the story through with them and perhaps rehearse some of the sounds and actions to make sure the characters they are going to create are clear in their minds before they start making. Perhaps it is a story of a scary monster stalking prey through the jungle. The children could imagine and demonstrate the noise of the monster's hot and smelly breath, its roar when it sights its prey and the scrabbling of its claws on the ground. They could produce the sounds of the jungle animals and build up the picture of the scene that the sounds painted in their imaginations.

Older people who are not used to the games played in playgrounds and rehearsal rooms may find it easier to begin the process with a discussion on a theme relevant to the project – relationships in the family perhaps or carbon footprints. Once people have started making the objects, they relax and more exciting theatre games can be developed. Couples can be encouraged to make their puppets talk to each other, or to walk about and meet the other puppets in the room. Whatever the method, the purpose remains the same – to make sure that everyone is clear about the goal they are working towards and has a part to play in making the end product.

The Planning

Any sort of workshop needs careful planning, particularly if children or amateur groups are involved. The same production decisions with regard to budget, timing and venue have to be made, but the angle of approach, particularly to the design and construction of puppets and objects, is different. A professional maker may struggle away in their workshop or studio experimenting, testing and throwing try-outs in the bin, but with group work it's better if things work out first time – or as near first time as can be managed. This only happens with careful design and rehearsal planning. However, the most carefully planned scheme must still allow space for the different levels of skills and commitment within the group.

Materials

Decisions about the realization of designs have to be made early enough to allow time to source and beg or buy the stuff to make them. A big part of this decision will depend on how much money there is to spend. The whole production may be made from waste products and coloured with the generous donations of the community's left-over house paint, or it may be built and painted with supplies ordered from specialist shops. Either of these methods takes time and forethought if the stuff is going to be ready and waiting for the first making-meeting. There is a certain advantage, when lots of different people are working on a project, to providing a limited range of materials. It is more interesting for everyone if they have the opportunity to create ideas from their own imaginations and the end result is more likely to coalesce if all the varied imaginations have the same materials to work with. It is a way of getting organization and chaos to work together.

A particular type of object can be chosen as the basis for all the puppets made in a session to ensure that they work as a group. It can be simple, such as wooden spoons or cardboard rolls, or more complicated, for example vegetable steamers or a collection of electrician's tools and equipment. Whatever is chosen will set a theme for all the work made in the session, but space must still be allowed for the inventive powers of the makers.

Following is a list of workshop essentials:

- sticks – garden centres are a good source of cheap sticks of differing lengths
- a small saw and craft knife for cutting sticks
- gaffer tape, masking tape, sellotape
- string
- paper
- card
- rubber bands

- rope
- strong threads
- wire and pliers
- scissors
- card
- glues of different types
- paint
- sewing equipment
- different fibres (wool, rope, fur, cord and so on to make hair).

Patterns

Patterns and templates may be necessary; if they are, make sure that they work before handing them over to the group. If you show a sample of the finished object it should not be too perfect or complete. Most people find it easier to make something if they have seen a three-dimensional example before they start, but your sample should not be a confidence-sapping marvellous creation which will make others doubt their own ability.

It is important to set the scale when making puppets. It is easy to assume that a group of people will work to the same scale, but people have differing natural tendencies to work small or huge. For instance, if the group is making a household of puppets, give a guideline for the intended scale of an adult male puppet; the finished puppets will then be more likely to look as if they belong in the same world.

Make the basic design and pattern simple and clear. It is easy to decorate and complicate later if people want to, but much harder to simplify and clean up the design of an object once it has been made. The most successful designs for community work have a fail-safe simplicity about them.

The lifespan of these puppets and objects is likely to be shorter than that of their profes-sional brothers, so though they have to be strong enough to last the course they will not be expected be as strong, durable and perfectly made.

Rehearsals

Professionals may lead the production, but most of the people taking part are doing it for fun and must fit it in with their busy daily lives. It is not their job, though it may be their favourite occupation, and it is not a step on the path to other work. The difference between the amateur and the professional is not necessarily a difference in skill and creativity; it is doing the work for love, for fun and for the good feeling and companionship it grows. The professional leading this process, who is used to people turning up on time and ready and paid to work, may find this difference exhausting and irritating, but it is to be respected and admired and used for all it is worth. Half the skill in organizing this sort of work is making a fail-safe plan that allows for the difference in commitment between the amateur and the professional, and the fact that the cast and crew choose to work with you rather than the other way round. And making sure that the organization makes things more, rather than less, fun.

THE THERAPEUTIC USE OF PUPPETS

The distance that exists between the puppet and its animator gives puppets a place away from public performance. They can go where angels fear to tread and walk confidently on ground that angels would sink in. A puppet could be allowed to share the inarticulate world of a disturbed child or a tongue-tied adult who would be unable to let another

Don Quixote fights the windmill – a community project.
TOP LEFT: *a meeting at the site.*
LEFT: *an early design and thoughts for construction.*
TOP RIGHT: *the puppets in action.*
Photos: Chris Baldwin

human share his or her thoughts. The puppet may not just be the questioner. It can also give unspeakable thoughts a voice and allow a troubled psyche to unload some of its burden. It can be a medium through which terrifying thoughts become manageable, fears can be faced and words can be spoken. It is as close to our instincts as biting and cuddling.

The success of the puppet as a mediator does not rely on the technical skill that goes into making or manipulating it. It can be as simple as a square of cloth rubber-banded round a ball of rolled-up paper, or a fork stuck into an apple, which can be given a character that is appropriate to the content of the discussion. A pillow could become a puppet to help young patients in hospital come to terms with the injections or other frightening treatments. Complicated subjects and emotional states that a child does not have the language to express can be played out and opened up through the use of a puppet.

Humans present a particular image of themselves. Everyone has other, less obvious, facets to their character which do not appear in public as often. There are times, of anger, depression or loneliness perhaps, when it can help if those facets are explored and acknowledged. These times of misfortune tend to revolve around a cycle of familiar situations and arrive back at their starting point. Talking about them can open a doorway out of the circle and show a new way of coping with a recurring situation. To make and play with, or have conversations with, another person through a puppet may unlock a new way out of this recurring dilemma. Three or four puppet versions of a person, each with a different emotional focus, make it possible to address a familiar situation in an innovative way. If the person makes their own puppets, however

inexpertly, the conversations will be easier and franker. Children find it easy to engage with this sort of activity, but an adult may feel as if they are playing silly games. The difficulty is in persuading people to begin to play; it is easy to talk frankly once the process has got going.

THE AUDIENCE

The familiarity audiences have of seeing performance through a screen has created a definite difference between stage and screen work. The days are past when films recorded something akin to a play in a theatre. Screened performance and performances seen live in theatres have become distant cousins rather than siblings. Their differences become obvious when watching a video of a theatre performance, which, however exciting it was in real life, appears flat and dreary through the lens.

Many writers, directors, designers and other theatrical inventors no longer have the same interest in trying to create a naturalistic appearance of reality onstage and trust the audience to interpret more abstract work. The camera lens is so much better at recording

It could happen like this ...

Adults are learning a foreign language. They are introverted and worried about making mistakes. They find it impossible to risk copying an accent so different to their own and cling to the rules of grammar rather than risk feeling foolish by trying to establish verbal communication with their partner in class. The teacher asks them to make puppets, just rough black paper silhouettes of each other, and to write a simple dialogue for the puppets to perform. These puppets are passed on to another couple so that no one in the class is using either their own face or their own dialogue. The couples rehearse and perform their duos with much less embarrassment and much more fluency. The puppet has freed them from their fear of looking foolish and allowed them to speak.

reality, and so omnipresent in society today, that there is little excitement for many people in seeing a live representation of real life on stage; they come to the theatre for a direct emotional, visual and intellectual experience which relies on their presence and interest to succeed.

Theatre audiences that have been exposed to contemporary theatre will be as adept at believing the extraordinary as a child. They will have no difficulty, if the genre demands it, in accepting a live mother producing a baby that is a puppet moving with the obvious assistance of another actress who produces its newborn wails and gurgles. They will enjoy the surprise of transformation and the power of the visual effects, accepting the reality of a puppet as easily as they do that of an actor.

Live performance has always been subject to change. These changes can seem new ideas – inventions and strokes of genius. In fact, like almost all performance, they are new combinations of old ideas recreated for the viewpoint of contemporary eyes. The skill and imagination that is used in puppetry and object theatre give some of the most exciting, inventive, innovative and delightful contemporary theatre. The dialogue between an audience and an animated puppet or object is unique. The audience knows that in order to become involved with the action, it must allow itself to believe that the beings onstage have human hearts and spirits. It must look at objects differently; scale and proportion and figurative movement must be discounted. What the audience agrees to see is the heart of the matter – the naked reality of feeling undisguised by the devices we use to make our daily emotional life less vivid, blatant and disturbing. The audience agrees to collude with the animators to experience the story.

The scope of the work stretches from performances designed for babies to explorations of the most intellectual nature. Puppets, shadows, objects and the visual invention that supports them produce the funniest, most inventive, most beautiful or plain bizarre performance you can see in theatres today. The most exciting practitioners are getting the chance to put their ideas into practice. The inventors of the work may employ nothing but a limited collection of found objects in a rudimentary set to tell a story or create a dreamlike world that transports members of the audience into a dimension outside their everyday lives. The phrase 'audience participation' calls up a picture of an active physical and vocal collaboration on the part of the audience. Object theatre is mental participation and, though the audience may be still and silent, it is participating in the action with as much vigour as the eight-year-olds shouting 'It's behind you!' at the pantomime.

Most important of all, it is bringing an audience back into auditoriums where all ages can experience the work together. In today's theatre actors, puppets, objects and animators can share the stage. Simple sets or fantastic visions form the background to the work and produce an atmosphere that draws the audience into the world of the performers – a world of puppets, light, sound, shadows and objects.

INDEX

143